MW01042910

Reproducible Activities

As a Matter of Fact

Nonfiction Reading Comprehension

Grades 5-8

By
Claudia Vurnakes

Cover Illustration by
Warner McGee

Inside Illustrations by
Kathryn Marlin

Published by Instructional Fair • TS Denison
an imprint of

McGraw-Hill Children's Publishing

About the Author

Claudia Vurnakes has been committed to the field of education for 20 years, with teaching experience at both middle and upper grade levels. She is the author of several teacher resource books in addition to easy readers, short story collections, and children's Bible study materials. Claudia lives in Wilmington, North Carolina, with her husband and two sons.

Credits

Authors: Claudia Vurnakes
Cover Artist: Warner McGee
Inside Illustrations: Kathryn Marlin

McGraw-Hill
Children's Publishing

A Division of The McGraw·Hill Companies

Published by Instructional Fair • TS Denison
An imprint of McGraw-Hill Children's Publishing
Copyright © 1999 McGraw-Hill Children's Publishing

Send all inquiries to:
McGraw-Hill Children's Publishing
3195 Wilson Drive NW
Grand Rapids, Michigan 49544

As a Matter of Fact—grades 5–8
ISBN: 1-56822-864-3

Table of Contents

Introduction

The biggest, the worst, the oddest, the unsolved—facts are packed with possibility. More than the wildest inventions of fiction, factual information draws us, because no matter how unlikely and obscure, we know a fact is something that actually happened. Amazing facts broaden our horizons; they help us to understand the infinite variety and detail in the world; they alert us to what might be hiding around the very next corner.

As a Matter of Fact brings the fascination of unusual information into your classroom. Here are odd tidbits that students love to ponder, each presented in a one- to two-page, concise unit containing vocabulary, comprehension, creative writing, and enrichment activities. Five thematic chapters provide something for every interest. "People to Ponder" will introduce students to some unique personalities most of us do not meet in the course of everyday life: an island baby sitter, a human cannonball, a geneticist who develops new vegetables. For the history nut, there is "Ancient Daze." Topics such as primitive beauty secrets or the inventions of the vending machine and the fire station pole point out amazing connections with cultures across the ages. "Master Disasters" will appeal to thrill seekers with accounts of the San Francisco earthquake, the black plague, the crash of the *Hindenburg*, and the Donner tragedy. And, since nature never fails to fascinate, "What in the World . . .?" and "Animal Magnetism" supply little-known information about porcupines, manatees, deserts, green skeletons, dirt, ears, lightning, prairie dogs, meteorites, and much more. With units on 78 different topics, *As a Matter of Fact* provides high interest along with the guided practice needed to sharpen vital skills in reading and responding.

This book is designed to challenge your fast workers and your divergent thinkers. Pull units in at random, or pursue a specific theme. Build a weekly vocabulary program based on these pages. Use them to extend your existing curriculum, to demonstrate interdisciplinary connections, to increase cultural literacy. Because of the variety of activities included in each unit, these pages are ideal for independent and group work keyed to different learning styles. Encourage students to keep a folder of their favorite units, to research and create new ones based on facts that personally fascinate them.

Thanks to the magic of media, students today have the opportunity to view much of the world's infinite variety and detail. We are indeed becoming a culture of watchers rather than doers. In a small way, *As a Matter of Fact* swims against the tide. Its pages encourage students to go beyond viewing alone, to stake out ownership of these amazing facts by engaging their powers of logic and imagination. "How does this fact relate to my life?" When students make information their own by asking questions such as this, they are well on their way to life-long learning.

Name _____

The U.S. Camel Corps

In the 1850s few Americans had an opportunity to see a real, live camel. For them, the camel bordered on the mythical, living only on the pages of exaggerated tales of foreign lands. Imagine the shock when wagon trains to the West encountered American soldiers on camelback, pacing across the Arizona desert. As strange as it seems, the exotic camel played a brief but vital role in the exploration and settlement of the Old Southwest.

Charged with opening a supply route from Texas to California, U.S. Army Major Henry Wayne faced a daunting challenge. He knew few horses could survive the rigors of the region, from snow-capped mountaintops to bone-dry, burning sand. What beast of burden, he wondered, could travel such great distances on the little food and water that would be available? That's when Major Wayne remembered the camel. It would eat almost any plant and could go four days before needing a drink. With its long, powerful legs and strong back, the camel could carry as much as 1,000 pounds of supplies over rocks and sand.

So Major Wayne went to Africa. There he purchased 33 camels and hired experienced men to train U.S. soldiers in the art of camel driving. The day the animals arrived in Indianola, Texas, townspeople hooted in derision. Had the army gone crazy, buying these beasts so strange-looking to American eyes? It was not long, however, before the camels proved their worth, successfully conveying much-needed cargo and mail to isolated army posts and small settlements.

Forty-two more camels were purchased and the U.S. Army Camel Corps was officially formed. Unique to this most unusual military unit was the horseman whose job was to ride ahead and prevent pandemonium by warning passersby, "The camels are coming! The camels are coming!"

Military officials wanted to expand the Camel Corps to cover the entire West, but the outbreak of the Civil War shelved those plans. By war's end, the railroad industry had grown large enough to handle western shipments. So the army sold off its camels, mostly to circuses and zoos. Twenty-eight were used for a package delivery service in the young settlement of Los Angeles. A few of the animals, however, escaped to the wilderness of Arizona. There, startled travelers over the next 60 years would occasionally spot the wild herd roaming free. As the camels grew old and died off, almost everyone forgot that, for a brief time, the pride of Arabia traversed the sands of the American West.

Name _____

The U.S. Camel Corps ➤

A. For each word write the letter of the correct definition.

_____ 1. mythical
_____ 2. exotic
_____ 3. daunting
_____ 4. rigor
_____ 5. derision
_____ 6. convey
_____ 7. pandemonium
_____ 8. traverse

a. to transport
b. to travel across
c. foreign and interesting
d. scorn, ridicule
e. intimidating, courage-draining
f. chaos
g. imaginary
h. extreme difficulty, harshness

B. Answer these vocabulary questions. You may need to use the back of this sheet.
   1. Circle the mythical characters: Ronald Reagan, Tooth Fairy, Porky Pig, Marilyn Monroe, Paul Bunyan.
   2. Explain how you could give yourself an exotic appearance.
   3. Of all your teachers, who is the most daunting? Why?
   4. What rigorous sport do you enjoy the most? Explain.
   5. Derision of each other appears to be some teens' favorite pastime. Explain.
   6. What message could you convey to your friends that would create pandemonium?

C. Place yourself in the shoes of one of the characters listed below. On the back of this sheet, write lines that he or she might have spoken.
   1. Major Wayne requesting money for camels from the government
   2. a citizen of Indianola, Texas
   3. a settler spotting a wild camel

D. Write T for true or F for false.

_____ 1. Horses probably reared and people panicked when the camels rode into view.

_____ 2. Major Wayne probably never visited a zoo or circus.

_____ 3. The U.S. government was not satisfied with the camels' job performance.

_____ 4. The Arizona desert was not a suitable habitat for the camel.

_____ 5. Western settlers depended on shipments from the East because they could not make everything they needed.

_____ 6. Major Wayne was very sensitive about others' opinions. He would quit rather than be laughed at.

_____ 7. Before Major Wayne began the corps, most of his men had most likely never seen a camel.

_____ 8. The Camel Corps had, at its largest, 1,000 beasts.

Name _____

Peacock Pilgrims

Most of us think of the Pilgrims as a gloomy bunch, attired from head to toe in shades of somber gray. But a study of their clothing, described by the Pilgrims themselves in wills and lists of household goods, shows that the exact opposite was true. The Pilgrims loved to wear bright colors!

The people who landed on the Massachusetts shore in 1620 were a diverse group of tradesmen, craft workers, and farmers united by a quest for religious freedom. Before leaving for the New World, they wore the clothing associated with their various occupations and social standings. William Bradford, who later served as governor of the Plymouth Colony, packed a red silk suit and a purple cape for the trip. Other Pilgrims brought along equally bright finery: green velvet breeches, mustard-colored overcoats and orange vests for the men, red and blue petticoats and scarlet slippers for the women. There was no "team" uniform or standard-color clothing required for passage on the *Mayflower*.

Once in the New World, the settlers took great care to prolong the life of their European-made garments. Who knew when the next ship bearing woven fabrics would arrive? Who knew how long it would be before the cobbler had leather and leisure to replace worn-out shoes? Clothes were very costly and hard to come by, but they were made to last, so the Pilgrims handed down valuable items to family members in their wills: "To my son James, I leave the sky-colored waistcoat and tawny breeches." "To daughters Samantha and Jane, a turkey-red petticoat each." Clothing colors mentioned by the Pilgrims include orange, violet, bright green, plum, yellow, light blue, red, and what was known as "mingled," or multicolored. In fact, the settlers' desire for colorful clothing grew so that, in the 1630s, their leaders felt it necessary to enact laws regulating excessive styles.

So where did the notion of gray-clad Pilgrims come from? It is not entirely wrong, merely a generation or two misplaced. Only after the colorful European clothing wore out did the Pilgrim wardrobes darken to home-dyed shades of gray, brown, dark green, and maroon, colors obtained from barks, berries, hulls, and roots. Years later, when prosperity finally came to the Massachusetts colony, Pilgrim families clung to their plain, dark clothing as a testimony of the simple lifestyle their parents had sought in coming to the New World.

Name _____

Peacock Pilgrims ⟶ ▼

A. Give the topic sentence of this selection. _____

_____

B. The rainbow is full of interesting color words. Write the basic color for each word listed here:
   1. indigo _____
   2. celadon _____
   3. sienna _____
   4. chartreuse _____
   5. umber _____
   6. vermilion _____
   7. dun _____
   8. cinnabar _____
   9. heliotrope_____
   10. azure_____
   11. ocher_____
   12. magenta_____

Now make a black-and-white drawing, coloring-book style, on a sheet of white paper. Label the sections of the drawing with the words above. Exchange drawings with a friend and color correctly.

C. Fill in the blanks below with these vocabulary words from the reading selection.

attired	prolong	clad
somber	garment	maroon
diverse	leisure	prosperity
occupation	notion	testimony

1. "Please give me the medicine now," the patient begged. "Do not _____ my agony."
2. We call the United States a melting pot because our citizens come from _____ ethnic backgrounds.
3. The man was found guilty of robbery, thanks to the _____ of his many victims.
4. Heavy clouds in the sky made it a _____ day.
5. Square dancing is a healthy _____ activity.
6. Every politician promises _____ and a better way of life to the voters.
7. The _____ occurred to Dr. Pasteur that heating milk would kill deadly germs.
8. _____ in suits and white shirts, the young men made quite an impression.
9. Choose an_____ that makes the most of your natural talents and abilities.
10. He felt sorry for the child shivering on his doorstep, _____ only in thin pajamas.
11. Before purchasing, try on the _____ to make certain it fits properly.
12. Chrysanthemums in shades of gold and _____ beautify the garden in autumn.

D. Which is better, to buy lots of inexpensive clothes that wear out quickly or to pay more for a few well-made clothes that last a long time? On the back of this sheet, defend your answer with at least three reasons.

E. Imagine that you have found an ancient cape folded up in an old trunk. You put the cape around your shoulders and, suddenly, scenes from Pilgrim days flash before your eyes. On another sheet of paper, write what happens.

Name _____

Father of Gadgets

Where would modern man be without his gadgets? There are gadgets to turn on the television, open the garage door, unscrew a jar lid, scoop up golf balls, curl eyelashes, and floss teeth. Small boys covet pocket knives loaded with gadgets; bigger boys dream of the Batmobile and the *Enterprise*. Born of man's ingenuity, small, handy tools have been around since the dawn of history. But we have called them *gadgets* only since 1886.

That was the year France presented the Statue of Liberty to the American people. A Monsieur Gaget, a French entrepreneur, cashed in on the big event by selling miniatures of Lady Liberty as souvenirs on the streets of Paris. Hundreds of visiting Americans brought home what they called "gadgets," mispronouncing the Frenchman's name in the process. The word stuck. Even though the original "gadget" had no function other than to make Monsieur Gaget some money, the word came to be applied to any small, handy device that makes everyday living easier.

A. Play a game of Categories with a partner. To prepare, secretly jot down gadget categories and list examples. Take turns calling out gadgets until one player correctly identifies his opponent's category. Here are some categories for starters: kitchen gadgets, beauty and grooming gadgets, sports gadgets, woodworking gadgets.

B. On another sheet of paper, design a homework machine loaded with every gadget imaginable to make doing your best work a pleasure.

C. Monsieur Gaget is in good company; many other people have contributed their names to common words in the English language. Use a dictionary or encyclopedia to learn more about these names-turned-words.
   1. sandwich   2. mesmerize
   3. maverick   4. bloomers
   5. poinsettia   6. leotard
   7. graham cracker   8. sideburns
   If your name became a household word, what would it most likely mean and why? On the back of this sheet, explain and give an example of your name used as a common noun in a sentence.

D. The Latin root GENS gives the meaning of "birth" to the word *ingenuity* used in the selection above. Ingenuity is the cleverness you are born with. GENS also includes the idea of "people, type" in its meaning. Search out and list at least 12 words built on this common root. Here's a start: *genesis, generation.*

_____

_____

_____

Name _____

S.O.S.

Cameras roll. On the movie set a mechanical lift jerks a tiny boat up and down as if it is caught in a storm. "SOS!" the captain barks into his radio. "Save our ship! Save our ship!" This episode would not occur in real life. Any sea captain worth his salt knows that the universal distress signal, SOS, does not mean "Save our ship."

Morse code was invented in 1835 as a way of transmitting messages by electricity. An internationally known artist, Samuel F. B. Morse, abandoned an illustrious career to develop the telegraph. He assigned a combination of short and long signals to each letter of the alphabet. In choosing an easy-to-remember, easy-to-send call for help, he decided on a combination of threes: three letters, with each letter composed of three signals. Of all the alphabet, only the letters S and O had three signals. Three dots stood for S; three longer signals, or dashes, stood for O. The call for help became SOS: short-short-short-long-long-long-short-short-short. This message, which stood for nothing other than "Help," has saved untold lives since its development.

A. Today we rely on many forms of communication: telephone, television, radio, e-mail, and fax machine. On a sheet of notebook paper, write a story about a modern situation in which Morse code would be the only means of communication available.

B. Look up International Morse Code. Encode on the back of this sheet the first message Samuel Morse ever sent by telegraph: "What God hath wrought!" Next, practice sending simple messages to a partner.

C. An acronym is a word formed from initials. It is a quick way of referring to a longer title. For each common acronym below, write the correct long form.
1. UNICEF _____
2. AWOL _____
3. VIP _____
4. radar _____
5. R.S.V.P. _____
6. OPEC _____
7. sonar _____
8. NASA _____
9. NATO _____
10. ZIP code _____

D. Research the life of Samuel F. B. Morse. Which do you think he cared more about, art or science? Why?_____
_____

E. Which contributes more to society: to paint beautiful art that hangs in museums or to invent a life-saving device? On another sheet of paper, take a stand and defend your point of view.

Name _____

For Vanity's Sake

Wrinkle cream of powdered antler, crocodile dung facials, rose petal lipstick, and fruit juice shampoo—since the dawn of time, people have used cosmetics to enhance their appearance. The ancient Egyptians applied blue-black color to their lips and stained their hands a stylish orange. Queen Jezebel of Old Testament fame used eye glitter made from the crushed shells of iridescent beetles. First-century Greeks favored a Neanderthal look, connecting their eyebrows above the nose in a heavy line of metal paste.

In nature, it is most often the male bird who displays the finer feathers. History shows that is also true for the male Homo sapiens. Jars of cream and cheek color, still sweet-smelling after 4,000 years, have been found in King Tutankhamen's pyramid tomb. Early Roman soldiers spent their final hours before battle having hair curled, nails painted, and perfume applied. They rubbed ground worms into the scalp for an overnight precaution against graying. Further north, the Saxons, early inhabitants of England, sported beards of bright blue, red, or green. French King Louis the Sixteenth powdered his hair pink, violet, or yellow—whatever complemented his outfit for the day.

Beauty, however, often came with a steep price. Many primitive procedures actually damaged the health of the wearer. The colorful paint American tribesmen smeared on their faces blocked and irritated the pores of their skin. Over time, permanent scarring resulted. The red coloring of Greek and Roman lip paint is known today to be especially harmful to an unborn child when absorbed into the mother's body. Countless miscarriages and birth defects occurred among wealthy women who unwittingly applied this beauty treatment on a regular basis. Medieval Europeans who desired whiter teeth coated them with nitric acid. The acid ate away layers of tooth enamel, yielding a brilliant smile—for a time. The result was massive tooth decay, infection, and agony. Dusting powders used through the 1700s were made from lead. Over years of powdering, the lead was absorbed into the bloodstream, where it caused organ damage and eventually death.

A look back at cosmetology through the ages suggests a question about the future: what bizarre beauty treatments will be fashionable in the twenty-first century?

For Vanity's Sake

Name _____

A. For each word write the letter of the correct definition.

_____ 1. facial
_____ 2. enhance
_____ 3. iridescent
_____ 4. Neanderthal
_____ 5. Homo sapiens
_____ 6. precaution
_____ 7. inhabitant
_____ 8. complement
_____ 9. primitive
_____ 10. cosmetology

a. to make something complete
b. the art of giving beauty treatments
c. care taken beforehand
d. rainbow-colored
e. a permanent resident
f. to intensify, to increase
g. from the earliest age
h. a beauty treatment for the face
i. the species man
j. pertaining to a type of primitive man

B. Write an original sentence for each word listed above, using the back of this sheet.

C. Give the topic sentence of this selection. What conclusion can you draw from this selection? Write it in your own words, using the back of this sheet.

D. Circle the best title for this selection.
 1. Good Looks Can Kill
 2. Ancient Beauty Secrets
 3. Male Peacocks Through the Ages
 4. Popular Makeup Colors

E. For each pair below, circle the treatment which came first in history.
 1. violet-powdered hair/beetle eye glitter
 2. blue beards/acid toothpaste
 3. soldier's nail polish/orange-dyed hands

F. For each quotation below, write a correct speaker.
 1. "Oh, no! The battle begins in ten minutes and my nails aren't dry!" _____
 2. "Darling, I dream about kissing your luscious blue lips!" _____
 3. "This bright green dye should scare those murderous Scots away!" _____

G. Give your answers on the back of this sheet.
 1. Why do humans enjoy changing their appearance?
 2. Design a new look that could answer the question in the last line of the selection.

H. Choose one. Research the role of cosmetics.
 1. Japanese Kabuki actors
 2. Native Americans

Name _____

Peking to Paris Proof ◢▼◣

When inventors built the first gasoline-powered automobiles, people regarded them as novelties, dangerous toys for rich thrill seekers. No one took seriously the suggestion that one day cars would replace horses as a reliable means of transportation. It took a 10,000-mile journey across two continents to convince the public of the automobile's future.

Although there were few motorists in Europe at the turn of the century, they yearned for a way to test their vehicles and newly acquired driving skills. So in 1901 the French newspaper *Le Matin* threw down a challenge: to race long distance, from Peking, China, all the way to Paris, France. Eager contestants plotted and planned for six years, but in the end only five cars entered the race. One was from the Netherlands; two were French-built, with engines equal to those of a modern-day motorboat; one was a six-horsepower three-wheeler; and the most powerful had a 40-horsepower engine. It was crewed by Italian Prince Scipione Borghese, an explorer and sportsman, along with his chauffeur and a reporter from Rome. Of all the car crews, Borghese made the most careful preparations. He measured mountain passes and shipped supplies ahead by camel to storage points along the route. To his auto he added extra fuel tanks, heavy-duty tires, and spare parts.

As a French army band played and firecrackers exploded, the five cars pulled out of Peking on June 10, 1907. Almost immediately, they encountered difficulties in the mountains between China and Mongolia. As coolies struggled with ropes to pull the cars up the peaks, camel trains strode smugly by. Next came the Gobi Desert, where engines boiled over daily in the intense heat. Here, the autos fared better, accomplishing in four days what usually took a caravan two weeks.

Studying their maps, the drivers looked forward to Russia, with the promise of well-traveled roads. But rains set in that washed out bridges and turned the country into a sea of mud. One of Borghese's metal wheels collapsed, threatening to end his quest, until a village carpenter, using only a hatchet, made a wooden replacement. Next, a mix-up with fuel shipments left Borghese stranded miles from the nearest gasoline. Oddly, a small shop beside the road had a large supply of benzine, a compound used in paint and dyes. With nothing to lose, Borghese dumped it into his tank and chugged off in a cloud of black smoke—all the way to his next supply point.

Once the drivers reached Europe, the difficulties eased. In fact, Borghese picked up so much speed, he was stopped in a Belgian town for exceeding the eight-mile-an-hour limit! Sixty-one days after leaving Peking, August 10, Borghese's crew limped into Paris. Only two other contestants finished, both arriving 20 days later. But their accomplishment proved to the world that the automobile could stand up to the most rigorous of driving conditions. The car was here to stay!

Peking to Paris Proof

Name _____

A. The solution to each clue below is a number from the reading selection.

1. Horsepower of Borghese's auto: _____
2. Continents crossed: _____
3. Years spent preparing for race: _____
4. Miles from Peking to Paris: _____
5. Days in which Borghese completed race: _____
6. Miles per hour in Belgian town: _____
7. Date the race was first proposed: _____
8. Number of contestants: _____
9. Days in which French drivers completed race: _____
10. Number in Borghese's crew: _____
11. Days required for camels to cross Gobi Desert: _____
12. Days in which automobiles crossed desert: _____

B. Reason and write. Use the back of this sheet.
1. What did this race most likely do for the newspaper that sponsored it?
2. Explain the effect this race may have had on a person considering the purchase of an automobile in 1907.

C. What happened first? Number the statements from 1 to 10 in chronological order.

_____ 1. Borghese breaks the speed limit.

_____ 2. Borghese fills up with benzine.

_____ 3. *Le Matin* proposes an auto race.

_____ 4. Engines boil over.

_____ 5. Only Borghese and two others finish.

_____ 6. Coolies pull the cars up the mountain peaks.

_____ 7. A few adventurers learn to drive.

_____ 8. Only Borghese and four others enter.

_____ 9. The crowd celebrates with firecrackers.

_____ 10. Many drivers consider taking up the challenge.

D. Create your own trail game of this auto race. On a large sheet of paper, draw a path of at least 50 game spaces. Use information from the selection to create at least 5 bonus spaces and 10 penalty spaces along the trail. (You will need to create additional details of your own.) Provide a penny for flipping to determine the number of spaces to move. (Ex.: heads = 1 space, tails = 3 spaces) Next, write the rules and supply game markers. Finally, test your game with a partner to see who reaches Paris first!

Name _____

Pole Position

After checking out the trucks, visitors to a fire station always ask to see it: The Pole, that slick, quick means of split-second travel from an upstairs bunkroom to fire engines below. But the pole did not originate with firefighters. Long before white colonists established the first fire departments, Aleut Indians of Alaska were using the pole to enter and exit their winter homes. To protect their families from long stretches of wet, snowy weather, the early Aleut built shelters partially underground. Called *barabaras*, these houses had earthen walls reinforced with whale bones. The roof was packed dirt and straw, and animal membranes were stretched across small openings to make translucent windows. A hole in the roof allowed smoke to escape and provided access to the pole, which was made from a tree trunk. Family members slid down to enter, then climbed back up the pole to exit.

A. For each word write the letter of the correct definition.

_____ 1. originate   a. a way to approach

_____ 2. reinforce   b. to begin

_____ 3. membrane   c. to strengthen or support

                        d. a thin, flexible layer of plant or animal material

_____ 4. translucent   e. letting partial light through

_____ 5. access

B. Answer these vocabulary questions.

1. How many means of access does your school building have? _____

2. From what part of the country does your family originate? _____

3. How can you tell if a piece of paper or cloth is translucent? _____

4. How does your family reinforce the rules of your school? _____

C. Think and answer, using the back of this sheet.
1. Using details from the reading selection, draw a diagram of a barabara. Label its features.
2. Explain ways a fire station pole would differ from the Aleuts' pole. Give reasons.
3. Explain the advantages *and* disadvantages of living in a barabara.

D. Imagine and write. Spin a tale explaining how the idea of the pole traveled from the wilds of Alaska to a big-city fire station.

E. Research these types of Native-American homes. How is each well-suited for its environment and culture?
1. the tipi (tepee)
2. the iglu (igloo)
3. the pueblo
4. the longhouse
5. the wickiup

Name _____

Sweet Kiss ────────────────────────────▼

"K-z-z-z-z, k-z-z-z-z." The machine steamed and hissed as it pushed dollops of dark, hot liquid out onto the moving belt. "It's working, Boss," a mechanic cried. "They're coming out, perfect as . . . as . . . kisses!"

Milton Hershey's bite-sized drops of milk chocolate first titillated American tastebuds in 1908. According to company archives, the candies were named for the distinctive sound made by the machine that formed the chocolate drops. Today over 12 billion Hershey's Kisses are consumed every year. At 25 calories a Kiss, that's a whole lot of love! Fifty-thousand cows produce 700,000 quarts of milk a day to keep the plant in Hershey, Pennsylvania, operating. There, the trip from raw cacao bean to milk chocolate is a short one, three to five days. The prepared chocolate enters the hissing Kissmaker, then travels down the cooling tunnel. In less than 18 minutes from start to finish, the candy is formed, cooled, and wrapped in silver foil. Thanks to a little Kiss, Hershey's commands the lion's share of the American candy market at 34 percent.

A. Write T for true or F for false.

_____ 1. More candy eaten in the United States is from Hershey's than from any other company.

_____ 2. It takes 700,000 cows to produce the milk the Pennsylvania plant needs.

_____ 3. The Kisses go from the drop machine directly to the wrapping station.

_____ 4. The story of how Kisses were named is a legend.

_____ 5. Americans have enjoyed Hershey's Kisses since the end of the nineteenth century.

B. Rube Goldberg was an inventor-turned-cartoonist. His humorous illustrations of complicated machines that did very simple tasks won him many fans. On the back of this sheet, draw and label the functions on your own Rube Goldberg-style Kiss machine.

C. The expressions below unite two objects that are alike in some special way. The phrase "lion's share" in the selection above tells us that Hershey's portion of candy sales is like the amount of food a lion eats, compared to the smaller, weaker animals of the jungle. On another sheet of paper, explain the meaning of each common animal expression here, then use it in an original sentence.

1. a bird's eye view
2. at a snail's pace
3. crow's feet
4. a dog's life
5. scarce as hens' teeth
6. wolf in sheep's clothing

D. Explain why the small size of the Hershey's Kiss is a key to the candy's popularity. List other foods that have followed this bite-size trend. _____

_____

_____

Name _____

The Travels of Plants

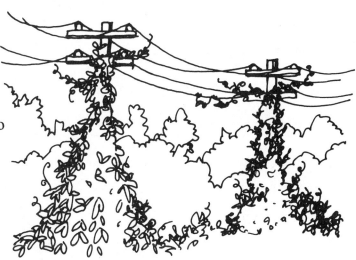

Ever thoughtful, Mother Nature provides travel plans for her rooted creations; plants spread to new locations thanks to wind, water, or animals. If the environment is right, the seeds or shoots gradually grow to fill the new territory. The process is slow but certain. When man steps in to aid these natural travel plans, the results are often mixed.

Take the apple, for example. This most loved of fruits originated in Turkey. Over centuries, through natural processes, apple trees began sprouting throughout the Mediterranean region. Roman soldiers dispatched to remote settlements in Europe and Africa packed apples as the perfect trail snack. They were easy to transport and lasted for weeks without spoiling. The soldiers munched as they marched, then tossed the cores along the wayside. The fruitful trees that sprang up behind them became known as "the stamp of Rome."

Everyone knows the charming story of how apples spread through the American wilderness. John Chapman, a Massachusetts orchardist better known as Johnny Appleseed, traveled throughout the Pennsylvania and Ohio territories to sow apple seeds along roads and river banks. What most people do not know is that Chapman also spread a weed that plagues farmers to this very day. A believer in herbal medicine, "Johnny Appleseed" scattered seeds of the dog fennel plant. Its leaves could be made into a treatment that would cool a high fever. Chapman did not realize that in the fertile wilderness soil, dog fennel would grow 15 feet tall and choke out everything else planted in a field. The farmers who battle dog fennel today call it "Johnnyweed."

Kudzu is another example of man's best plant intentions going awry. This fast-growing vine was discovered in the Orient, climbing luxuriantly up walls and posts. Its long, nitrogen-producing roots enriched the soil and kept it from eroding. American experts saw in this Oriental plant a way to restore farms in the South exhausted from years of cotton- and tobacco-growing. The vine would also provide good fodder for livestock, they reasoned. So in the 1930s, encouraged by experts, southern farmers planted kudzu. What no one realized was that the South lacked the cold winters that in China and Japan cut kudzu down to size. With year-round mild temperatures, kudzu took off and never stopped. Today it hangs like a heavy green curtain from telephone poles, power lines, and trees all over the South, blocking vision and choking out other plants. Thousands of dollars are spent each year to control a vine brought in to help, not hurt.

Should man leave the spreading of plants strictly in the hands of Mother Nature? No, for certainly there are success stories, such as the Roman soldiers and their apples. Should man think carefully before introducing growing things to a new environment? Unless we want more Johnnyweed and kudzu, most definitely!

The Travels of Plants

Name _____

A. Circle the best title.
1. An Apple a Day
2. Plant Mistakes
3. Apples and Kudzu
4. Kudzu Boo-boo
5. Transplantation Explanation

B. On the back of this sheet, give the topic sentence for this selection. Explain the conclusion in your own words.

C. Write T for true or F for false.

_____ 1. Roman soldiers packed apples in order to plant orchards.

_____ 2. Kudzu is a thin vine with few leaves spaced widely apart.

_____ 3. Dog fennel has healing properties.

_____ 4. Johnny Appleseed accidentally spread dog fennel as he planted apple seeds.

_____ 5. Once planted, kudzu does nothing beneficial for the soil.

_____ 6. Planting a single crop year after year wore out the southern soil.

_____ 7. John Chapman brought apples to the American West Coast.

_____ 8. Chapman was experienced in planting apple trees prior to his wanderings.

_____ 9. Kudzu remains a manageable size in Japan.

_____ 10. Turkish travelers planted apples throughout Mediterranean countries.

D. Choose one of these titles and write an original short story on notebook paper. Make plants the focus of your story.
1. Kudzu Creature
2. Johnny Appleseed's Journal
3. Rome on the March

E. Match each clue with the correct answer. You may use an answer more than once.

_____ 1. Johnny Appleseed's real name
_____ 2. place where apples first grew
_____ 3. keeps kudzu small
_____ 4. cured by dog fennel
_____ 5. currently requires much cutting back
_____ 6. effectively prevents erosion
_____ 7. makes a good feed for cows and horses
_____ 8. place where kudzu first grew
_____ 9. lacked medicinal plants
_____ 10. Johnnyweed

a. kudzu
b. fevers
c. dog fennel
d. Turkey
e. dog fennel and kudzu
f. China and Japan
g. freezing temperatures
h. John Chapman
i. settlers in Pennsylvania and Ohio

Name _____

The Mysterious Smile

Hers is perhaps the most famous smile in all the world. Everyone who sees it wonders: what is the reason for that intriguing expression? Exactly what is she looking at, just beyond your right shoulder? Leonardo Da Vinci's painting *La Gioconda,* better known as the *Mona Lisa,* has fascinated people ever since the artist first began work on it around the year 1500. Thousands flock to Paris each year to see Da Vinci's original oil. Schools and galleries all over the world display copies. Modern advertisers even use her smile to sell their products. But for all her familiarity, there is much about the haunting *Mona Lisa* shrouded in mystery.

We do know her identity. She was Lisa Gherardini, the 21-year-old wife of a wealthy Italian merchant, Francesco del Giocondo. The affluence of Lisa's husband raises the first mystery: Why did Lisa choose to wear such dark, plain clothing for her portrait? Other women of her class preferred sumptuous dresses and jewels. Perhaps Da Vinci chose simple clothes that would not detract from Lisa's interesting face. Another possibility is that the young woman was in mourning. Church records show that the family had experienced the death of their baby a few months prior to commissioning this portrait. Could Lisa's sad smile be all about memories of her child?

The artist himself was well-acquainted with sadness, although it was of a different nature. History records that Leonardo Da Vinci had frequent disputes with those who hired him. They wanted the fruit of his brilliant mind—the paintings, the military inventions, the plumbing, and the canals—but they did not understand when a project took longer or cost more than what they had planned. This lack of understanding made the artist a lonely man. Is this something Mona Lisa perceived as Leonardo painted?

Another mystery is that Da Vinci worked to perfect this picture for more than six years but then never relinquished it to the family. Instead the painting ended up in the possession of the king of France. Why? Art historians hold many theories. Perhaps Lisa's husband simply disliked the finished portrait. Maybe Da Vinci, desiring compensation for six years' worth of work, set the final price too high. Another good guess is that the artist himself had fallen in love with the painting and refused to give it up, taking it with him when he went to work for the French court. It is well-known that, once in France, Leonardo painted almost nothing. His hands were showing signs of the paralysis that plagued his final years, and King Francis had other plans for him, as well. Busy designing his amazing machines, did Leonardo keep the *Mona Lisa* near simply so he could enjoy his last great work for himself?

Unless new information comes to light, we probably will never know the answer to the *Mona Lisa* mysteries. But the lady herself will go on smiling, as she has through the ages, bringing wonder and pleasure to people everywhere.

The Mysterious Smile

Name _____

A.   For each word write the letter of the correct definition.

_____	1.	shrouded	a. to know instinctively, without being told
_____	2.	identity	b. to give up one's claim
_____	3.	sumptuous	c. covered, hidden from view
_____	4.	dispute	d. to answer a riddle or explain a problem
_____	5.	perceive	e. luxurious, costly
_____	6.	relinquish	f. to be tormented by a persistent problem
_____	7.	theory	g. the facts about a specific person
_____	8.	compensation	h. argument
_____	9.	plagued	i. a guess or opinion, not fact
_____	10.	resolve	j. payment

B.   Fill in the blanks below with the vocabulary words.

1. _____ over countries' border lines have caused many a bloody battle.
2. In the well-known Bible story, "The Prodigal Son," a father prepares a _____ feast for his returning son.
3. Christopher Columbus was among the first to test the _____ that the world was round.
4. _____ by heavy fog, the ship anchored in the harbor was almost invisible.
5. A good job honestly done deserves fair _____.
6. She was _____ with frequent bouts of seasickness on her first ocean voyage.
7. Why is it mothers can so often _____ their children's deepest thoughts?
8. "Young man, I _____ my daughter to you. See that you help her be happy," the bride's father said.
9. With his keen powers of observation, Sherlock Holmes could _____ the most baffling mysteries.
10. His unusual voice gave the masked man's _____ away.

C.   On the back of this sheet, list all the mysteries mentioned in this selection about the *Mona Lisa*. You should find four or more. Next, suggest answers to these questions. Who knows? You just might hit on some solutions!

D.   Write as Lisa, Leonardo, or Francesco, and reveal a fact no one has known about the famous painting. _____

_____

_____

_____

Name _____

Pie in the Sky ◤▼

In the early 1900s, the Frisbie Bakery of Bridgeport, Connecticut, sold pies baked in metal pie plates. Yale University students, frequent buyers of the pies, would let off steam by flinging their empty pie tins across the campus yard. A sudden shout of "Frisbie!" was a signal that all pedestrians in the vicinity who valued their heads should duck. But that was not the first appearance for the flying disk. Archaeologists have found antecedents for the popular plaything in both Greek and Native-American cultures. Athletes competing in the Olympic Games of ancient Greece hurled the discus, a flat, round plate of stone weighing about three pounds. On the other side of the globe, Northwestern Indians challenged each other in contests of distance and accuracy using platter-shaped baskets woven of reeds. When the plastic Frisbee exploded on the American scene in the 1960s, people of all ages gave it a whirl. With a museum of its own in Seattle, Washington, and millions of afficionados, the Frisbee has proven itself to be more than just pie in the sky!

A. Match these vocabulary riddles with the correct answers.

_____ 1. A sun-darkened afficionado is . . . .   a. a near ear

_____ 2. A pedestrian who loves to chat is . . . .   b. "Pitch 'n' Itch"

_____ 3. A hearing organ in your vicinity is . . . .   c. an early girlie

_____ 4. A contest requiring accuracy of both eye and hand is . . . .   d. a tan fan

_____ 5. An antecedent of modern womanhood is . . . .   e. a good-aim game

_____ 6. A game in which players hurl handfuls of poison   f. a walkie talkie
ivy is called . . . .

B. Plan a day-long Frisbee Fun Festival of wacky games and activities, all of which use a Frisbee. Example: Serve refreshments on Frisbee "plates." On the back of this sheet, list at least 12 activities.

C. Write a mini-mystery using one of these titles:
1. The Case of the Forgotten Frisbee
2. Frisbee Fright Night
3. Frisbee on the Frontier

D. Invent a new game using some cast-off item or leftover. Come up with a clever name and a marketing strategy. Demonstrate your game for the class.

E. Research the origin of one of these common playthings.
1. the yo-yo
2. the hula hoop
3. marbles
4. the kite

Name _____

Hero's Army

Like an army of steadfast soldiers, coin-fed machines stand and deliver. Thousands guard parking spaces, countless others dispense soft drinks, candy bars, or bubble gum, some provide inquisitive tourists a telescopic view of picturesque scenery. Slot machines, better-known as "one-armed bandits," gobble gamblers' money.

Most mechanical coin-in-the-slot machines make use of lever action. A coin placed in a slot falls down to trip a lever inside the machine. The lever pushes open some type of door or valve to release a product or move a gauge. These machines can trace their ancestry all the way back to the first century A.D. A man named Hero, one of the most prolific inventors of all time, devised a holy water dispenser for a sanctuary in Alexandria, Egypt. Patrons inserted their coins in an opening at the top of a large urn, then held cups under a spout at the base to catch the water that was released. Little did Hero know his was only the first of an entire army of vending machines that would eventually take over the world!

A. On a separate sheet of paper, diagram the inner workings of a coin-fed machine based on information from the selection.

B. In addition to the vending machine, Hero is credited with inventing the first steam engine and the screw press. Research to learn more about Hero's work.

C. Write a short science fiction thriller for one of these titles.
   1. Revenge of the Slot Machines
   2. Parking Meter Plot
   3. Time Travel on a Dime
   4. Hero's Return

D. Answer these vocabulary questions on the back of this sheet.
   1. Of what store are you a *patron*? Explain.
   2. When you daydream, what *picturesque* scene most often comes to mind?
   3. What can you obtain from *vendors* at local athletic events?
   4. Who *dispenses* the best advice in your family and why?
   5. During what time of day is your mind its most *prolific*? Explain.
   6. Why are most small children *inquisitive* during the month of December?
   7. List at least four things you might do with an *urn*.

E. How many ways do vending machines serve you? Go through an imaginary day and list as many uses as possible. Write your list on the back of this sheet.

Name _____

The Lost State of Franklin

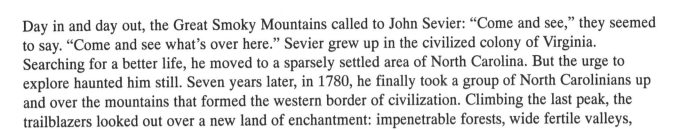

Day in and day out, the Great Smoky Mountains called to John Sevier: "Come and see," they seemed to say. "Come and see what's over here." Sevier grew up in the civilized colony of Virginia. Searching for a better life, he moved to a sparsely settled area of North Carolina. But the urge to explore haunted him still. Seven years later, in 1780, he finally took a group of North Carolinians up and over the mountains that formed the western border of civilization. Climbing the last peak, the trailblazers looked out over a new land of enchantment: impenetrable forests, wide fertile valleys, rushing streams, and, in the air above it all, a smoky blue mist that spoke of mystery and magic.

Sevier and his men rushed home to bring their families back, to create the perfect life of which they had dreamed. For a time, peace reigned. The settlers trapped large numbers of furs, which they sent back over the mountains. But angry disputes with the Cherokee Indians broke out in 1784, and Sevier wrote home for help. He was baffled when the new state government of North Carolina refused to send military aid. Why wouldn't the state help its own people?

Preoccupied with the difficulties of growing from a dependent colony into an independent state, North Carolina took no action. The new government had its hands full managing the populated portions of the state. What help could Sevier's settlers realistically expect, state leaders asked, when they had moved so far from civilization?

Spurred by North Carolina's brush-off, John Sevier and his followers declared their settlement to be a state in its own right. They wrote their own constitution and elected Sevier as their first governor. Hoping to join the United States as quickly as possible, they sought the backing of Benjamin Franklin, even naming their state in his honor.

No one knew what to do about the tiny new state of Franklin, way over on the other side of the mountains. While the North Carolina state and federal governments argued, the new citizens of Franklin had fun creating their own laws and institutions. What with the beautiful, misty land and the ideal government in place, they knew Franklin would be like heaven on earth.

But this paradise did not last long. In 1789 the federal government rejected Franklin's statehood. Undaunted, Sevier and his people kept lobbying. At last, in 1796, what had been Franklin was merged with other territory to become Tennessee, the sixteenth of the United States. Life went on much as before, and it was good. But for those who had dreamed of living in a perfect place, a state of their own called Franklin, nothing would ever be quite the same.

The Lost State of Franklin

A. What happened first? Number the statements from 1 to 5 in chronological order.

_____ 1. North Carolina refused to help the settlers over the mountains.

_____ 2. The national government refused Franklin's attempt to become a state.

_____ 3. Franklin became part of Tennessee.

_____ 4. Sevier was elected governor.

_____ 5. Sevier wanted to cross the Smoky Mountains.

B. For each quotation, write the correct speaker.

1. "What? They have named a state after me? In Heaven's name, why?" _____

2. "They left here four years ago. So why should we help them now?" _____

3. "Oh, my dear! It is as lovely as you said it would be!" _____

4. "There are too many people around here. I need some air." _____

C. Every state, even the lost state of Franklin, needs a state flag and a state song. On another sheet of paper, draw an appropriate banner and write new words to a familiar tune in honor of "the state that was."

D. The citizens of Franklin jumped at the opportunity to create new and better laws. If you could wipe the slate clean and write just ten laws for our country, what would they be and why? Write your list on the back of this sheet.

E. These sentences contain vocabulary words from the reading selection. Mark each C for correct or I for incorrect usage.

_____ 1. The players were *undaunted* by their opponents' jeers and catcalls.

_____ 2. Unfortunately, weapons manufacturers have developed bullets that can pierce vests that were once thought *impenetrable*.

_____ 3. Math just *baffles* me; I love nothing more than untangling a juicy word problem!

_____ 4. "I've never seen such a *sparse* head of hair," the stylist exclaimed as she struggled to comb the child's hair.

_____ 5. His good composition grade *spurred* him on to write about other local issues.

_____ 6. Our student council *lobbied* for longer lunch periods—and lost.

F. The idea of a perfect place now lost to man is a common theme in literature. Research to learn more about these dream spots.

1. the Garden of Eden
2. Shangri-La
3. Atlantis
4. Utopia

Name _____

Tulipomania

It was the year 1632 and, all across the Netherlands, cupboards were bare. The few families who had money to spend could find little food to buy, even at exorbitant prices. An entire country was in crisis, all because of tulipomania.

An explorer to Turkey sent the first tulip bulbs back to Europe in 1550. The flowers flourished in royal gardens and, within five years, wealthy families in France, England, and Germany enjoyed growing solid-colored tulips. Thirty-eight years later, tulips finally reached the gardens of commoners. A German university professor brought bulbs to Holland to sell, the high price enhancing their appeal. The bright blooms that sprouted from onion-like bulbs delighted the Dutch, and soon tulips grew in gardens all over the country. As the flowers became more common, bulb prices fell until the day a plant virus attacked a single flower bed, producing the first striped tulips the world had ever seen. Overnight, prices skyrocketed.

Rich and poor alike spent their life savings for infected bulbs. One single, multicolored bulb brought in trade 36 bags of corn, 72 bags of rice, 4 cows, 12 sheep, 8 pigs, 2 barrels of wine, 4 barrels of beer, 2 tubs of butter, 2 pounds of cheese, and a silver cup—over $70,000 in today's currency. Farmers abandoned food crops to cultivate the flowers. Bakers ran out of flour; produce markets were barren. The story is told of a housewife who prepared a stew using all she had on hand, bulbs. Only after enjoying the meal did her husband discover he had eaten $500,000 worth of bulbs.

By 1637 the flower fanciers of Holland had developed a rainbow of striped, feathered, and marbled tulips. The government stepped in at last and set strict price limits for the bulbs. With the stroke of a pen, fortunes were lost and farmers went bankrupt. But the public never got over its love affair with the tulip. Holland's economy slowly recovered with steadily increasing bulb sales to gardeners around the world.

By World War II, the Netherlands was exporting over 100 million bulbs a year to the United States alone. But the hardships of the war years once again found the Dutch without enough food to eat. Rather than watch families starve, many growers donated their stock of valuable bulbs to their neighbors' stewpots.

Name _____

Tulipomania ▼

A. These sentences contain vocabulary words from the selection. Mark each C for correct or I for incorrect usage.

_____ 1. His *exorbitant* lifestyle of parties and drugs finally cost him his life.
_____ 2. Many allergy-sufferers who move to the Southwest *flourish* in the dry, clean air.
_____ 3. A wise king will always seek the support of the *commoners*.
_____ 4. "You should not wear red, darling. It *enhances* your aging, bloodshot eyes."
_____ 5. Travelers overseas must convert their cash into the local *currency* if they wish to buy souvenirs.
_____ 6. She was *abandoned* by her children's behavior in public.
_____ 7. The purpose of education is to *cultivate* the student's academic strengths and remedy his weaknesses.
_____ 8. Row after row of tall, healthy corn grew in the *barren* fields.
_____ 9. "No, a book on homing pigeons would only bore me," sighed the bird *fancier*.
_____ 10. "I will *donate* this valuable painting to you for the small price of $1,000,000."

B. On the back of this sheet, make a time line for the five dates mentioned in this selection. Decide what may have happened in the years 1500 and 1645. Beside each date, place a plus or minus sign to show whether the price of tulips was rising or falling.

C. In times of food shortage, the Dutch ate tulip bulbs. On another sheet of paper, formulate a plan. What could your family do to prepare for a severe food shortage in this country due to war or economic crisis?

D. On a separate sheet of paper, draw your own designer tulip, then write an ad describing its rare features.

E. Flowers that bloom and die after one growing season are called *annuals*. *Perennials* bloom for several seasons, sometimes even years. Research to list five kinds of annual flowers and five perennial ones. _____

F. On the back of this sheet, name three recent products which have triggered buying crazes. What made these items so desirable that people would rush to purchase them?

G. The words *mania* and *phobia* are opposites. *Mania* is a craze or irrational love of something; *phobia* is the intense, sick fear of an object or activity. The two words appear as suffixes in the list below. Use a dictionary to define these common manias and phobias on a separate sheet of paper.

1. pyromania
2. kleptomania
3. Anglomania
4. Beatlemania
5. hydrophobia
6. claustrophobia
7. agoraphobia
8. photophobia

Name _____

Brick by Brick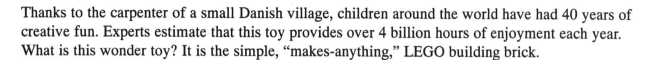

Thanks to the carpenter of a small Danish village, children around the world have had 40 years of creative fun. Experts estimate that this toy provides over 4 billion hours of enjoyment each year. What is this wonder toy? It is the simple, "makes-anything," LEGO building brick.

Understanding the influences that shaped this toy requires a trip back to simpler times. Ole Kirk Christiansen supplied everything wooden that was needed in the small farming community of Billund, Denmark. He built houses and furniture, ironing boards, and stepladders. A man of deep faith, he built Billund's church during World War I, when the shortage of materials caused him to lose a great deal of money on the job. But no matter what the difficulty, Ole tried to live by his company motto: Only the Best Is Good Enough. To fine tune his designs and eliminate waste, the carpenter frequently made miniature models of his wooden projects. It was a simple step from tiny ironing boards to an assortment of wooden toys. Children loved the colorful playthings on wheels; parents—even the poor farmers of Billund—appreciated the excellent value Ole provided at a reasonable cost.

With World War II came the introduction of a new material, plastic. Ole was paying attention. He began making traditional stacking blocks from this new plastic when he realized it offered more possibilities. Keeping the small, brick shape, Ole added studs to the top of the block, enabling it to connect to another block placed on top. He called his creation "the automatic binding brick."

As many a pioneer knows, trailblazing is always difficult. The first stores to receive boxes of LEGO bricks returned them unsold. Few people looking at the box covers could understand how to use the bricks inside. That's when Ole's grandson Kjeld first got involved in the company. Ole brought in a photographer to capture young Kjeld and his sisters at play, creating buildings and bridges from the blocks. (Sets did not include wheels at this time.) These pictures went on the front of the LEGO boxes and sales began to climb. Slowly, children in Denmark, Sweden, and Norway discovered the endless fun offered by Ole's building system. Once the toy succeeded in Germany, Europe's leading toy manufacturing nation, the Christiansen family knew they had a winner.

Today, Ole's grandson Kjeld presides over a company that has set lofty standards for the playsets it produces. In immaculate factories located in Denmark, Switzerland, Brazil, Korea, and the United States, bricks meet drop tests, twist tests, bite tests, size tests, and poison tests, all performed by machine. Since hundreds of pieces go into each set, computers provide a counting system that eliminates human error. The one place you will see plenty of people is in the design department. What looks like child's play is actually very demanding work, making certain that every new idea still lives up to Ole's motto.

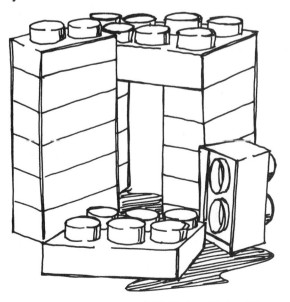

Name _____

Brick by Brick ▬▬▬▬▬▬▬▬▬▬▬▬▬▬▬▬▬▬▬ ▼

A. Write T for true or F for false.

_____ 1. Ole made and sold wooden toys when he first became a carpenter.
_____ 2. Ole was one of the first to make toys of plastic.
_____ 3. LEGO plants require hundreds of workers to tend the equipment.
_____ 4. From the first bricks made, LEGO playsets were a huge success.
_____ 5. Ole was not much good at making adult-size ladders and ironing boards.
_____ 6. In the 1940s Germany led Europe as the leading toy manufacturer.
_____ 7. Ole believed in making a profit even if he had to cut back on quality.
_____ 8. The LEGO company is still led by the Christiansen family.
_____ 9. Manufacturing LEGO bricks is a dirty job.
_____ 10. Without the development of plastic, the LEGO brick would never have been
         created.

B. Ole Kirk Christiansen based his decisions and actions in life on a motto. Choose one of the
    mottoes below and explain on the back of this sheet how it could apply to a real situation in
    your life.
    1. Anything worth doing is worth doing right.
    2. A stitch in time saves nine.
    3. A bird in the hand is worth two in the bush.
    4. Inch by inch, life's a cinch.

C. Think and answer.
    1. What makes the LEGO brick system such a good toy? Give at least ten reasons of your
        own.
    2. Today LEGO sets come with wheels, gears, batteries, motors, lights, and magnets. Make
        some predictions about the additions the company should make for the twenty-first
        century.
    3. Get two, eight-stud LEGO bricks and experiment. How many different ways can you
        stack the blocks together?

D. Choose one of the titles below and write a short story featuring LEGO bricks.
    1. Lift-Off to LEGOland
    2. Yo, ho, ho and a Keg o' LEGO!
    3. With the Click of a Brick
    4. Model Madness

E. In an encyclopedia read about Ole Kirk Christiansen's fellow Dane, Hans Christian Andersen.
    In what ways were the two men similar? How did they differ?

Name _____

Code-Talkers ——————————————————▼

It was 1944, and the war in the Pacific was not going well. The Japanese showed an uncanny ability to turn up in locations that the Americans had guarded as top-secret. Casualties soared and the number of defeats climbed steadily. In desperation, U.S. military officials searched for the leak. But no turncoat was found. The problem boiled down to codes. No matter what secret code the American forces used, the clever Japanese found a way to break it. Instructions radioed to American units hidden on tiny atolls were intercepted and decoded by the enemy almost as quickly as they were sent. The problem seemed unsolvable. Then a young Navajo serviceman made a plausible suggestion. Why not relay messages in the language of his people? Theirs was an unusual language that thwarted most nonnative learners. How many Japanese soldiers could possibly speak Navajo?

The generals decided the idea was worth a try. With a Navajo soldier manning the radio at each end, the first message was transmitted in the unique Native-American language. Nothing happened—no enemy troop movements, no planes overhead. The Japanese had been unable to decipher the message. With that success, more than 2,000 stalwart Navajo stepped forward. They were dispatched to some of the most dangerous battlefields of World War II to relay top-secret instructions. Thanks to the efforts of the men known as the Navajo Code-Talkers, the war in the Pacific was won.

A.   Research to answer these questions about the Navajo tribe.
   1.   Why were the Navajo able to retain so much of their land?
   2.   Why does that land make the Navajo one of the wealthiest tribes in America?
   3.   What do the Navajo call themselves?
   4.   What is the purpose behind the Navajo sand paintings?

B.   For each word write the letter of the correct definition.
   ____ 1. uncanny   a. to translate from code
   ____ 2. casualty   b. brave, stout-hearted
   ____ 3. turncoat   c. loss due to death
   ____ 4. atoll   d. to frustrate or defeat
   ____ 5. plausible   e. mysterious, weird
   ____ 6. thwart   f. a traitor
   ____ 7. decipher   g. to send on official business
   ____ 8. dispatch   h. a coral island
   ____ 9. stalwart   i. reasonable, with a good chance for success

C.   For each clue, write the letter of the correct rhyming pair.
   ____ 1. a reptilian turncoat   a. bold mold
   ____ 2. to frustrate a skin growth   b. a Nile isle
   ____ 3. a strange baby sitter   c. possible fossils
   ____ 4. stalwart slime   d. to thwart a wart
   ____ 5. an atoll in an Egyptian river e. a gator traitor
   ____ 6. plausible prehistoric artifacts f. an uncanny nanny

Name _____

If the Shoe Fits

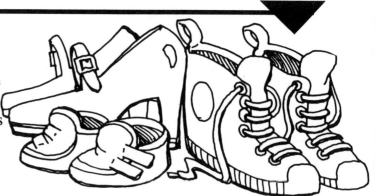

Whether high-tech sneakers or glamorous high heels, the shoes we choose to wear are much more than basic protection for our feet. Today's shoes broadcast our gender, our style, our status. Perhaps that has always been true, but history provides very practical reasons for the development of various shoe styles.

The first high heels helped hold horseback riders' feet securely in stirrups. They also offered elevation from waste-strewn streets in a time when chamberpots were routinely dumped from bedroom windows. Three-inch heels helped French King Louis XIV disguise his lack of stature; from then on, stylish men and women wore them. The tassels on your loafers are a hand-me-down from early hunters who adorned their boots with the small paws or tails of the animals they had snared, a clever way to advertise their prowess. If the ridges on the bottom of your gym shoes look like tire treads, it is because the synthetic rubber used was developed by tire manufacturer Charles Goodyear. He offered his product to the makers of galoshes, who first glued it to the soles of leather shoes and later canvas ones. The Velcro that today keeps tiny tots from tripping over loose laces grew out of one man's effort to copy the prickly seedpods that stuck to his clothes when he walked in the woods.

From flashing lights to Flubber, no one knows the next big news in shoes. What we do know, however, is that we will always make certain our feet travel in style.

A. For each word, write the letter of the correct definition.
- _____ 1. status   a. skillfulness
- _____ 2. securely   b. standing in the community
- _____ 3. strewn   c. trapped
- _____ 4. snared   d. firmly in place
- _____ 5. prowess   e. shoes worn in wet weather
- _____ 6. galoshes   f. scattered

B. On another sheet of paper, answer these vocabulary questions.
1. At what ceremonies are flowers frequently strewn?
2. In what skill do you exhibit prowess? Explain.
3. Give three good ways to snare a sweetheart.
4. Which students at your school have status and why?
5. During which months of the year are galoshes most often needed?
6. What products will hold a poster securely to the wall?

C. Choose one of the historic shoes from the selection and create an ad for it. Come up with a catchy name and promote the benefits of the shoe. Use the back of this sheet.

D. Predict the next big shoe trend. Illustrate your prediction on another sheet of paper.

Name _____

Chuckwagon Wonder

"The way to a man's heart is through his stomach!" The old maxim was never more true than along America's great cattle trails. Western ranchers depended on cowboys to lead huge herds of cattle across the plains to rail stations for shipment East. It was a grueling job, and the men who drove the herds were a unique breed—tough as rawhide, ornery as mules, mean as rattlesnakes. The one thing ranchers could do to ensure the success of a trail drive was to provide good "grub" or "chuck," cowboy slang for food. A well-fed cowboy was usually a loyal, hard worker.

The cook, known by such monikers as "Cookie," "Doughroller," "Biscuit-shooter," or "Grub-wrangler," was often a man too old or physically unsuited for work on horseback. Instead, he drove a wagon outfitted with three months' worth of food ahead of the herd each day. His job was to set up camp and have a hot meal ready when as many as 30 men arrived at sundown. With limited supplies and under arduous conditions, the cook turned out huge quantities of flapjacks, frying-pan bread, son-of-a-gun stew, sowbelly (bacon) and beans, slumgullion (beef stew), and coffee—the hotter, blacker, and thicker, the better.

As crucial as good food was to every trail drive, the cook also performed other valuable functions. As the advance man, he kept his eyes open for water and places where horses could graze. He was often the first to meet up with Indians or robbers, and his single-handed efforts with a rifle frequently saved the whole crew from danger. He patched up the men and tended them when they received injuries; he led prayers and buried them when they died. But it was his personality that provided the greatest asset. Whether a clown, a grouch, or a surrogate dad, he was the one to welcome lonely men home at the end of a long, hard day.

Wheezing into a harmonica or strumming on a battered guitar, the best "cookies" could offer entertainment of sorts. Some became skilled storytellers, stretching adventures of the trail into outlandish yarns. Others wrote humorous or sentimental verse that recalled the pleasures of home. A few even led their men in song, creating the country-western sound that remains popular to this day. For a rancher hoping to see large profits from a successful trail drive, the salary for the right cook was money well-spent.

Name _____

Chuckwagon Wonder ➤

A. Some of the sentences below are true, and some go too far to be true all the time. Place a check beside the sentences that are correct. Place a plus sign beside the sentences that claim too much.

_____ 1. Being a chuckwagon cook was almost always a dangerous job.
_____ 2. Being a trail cook brought out the best in a man.
_____ 3. Every crew treated its cook with courtesy.
_____ 4. The quantity of food was much more important to each cowboy than the quality.
_____ 5. The cook and his chuckwagon provided the only home men had while on the trail.
_____ 6. "Grub-Wrangler" was used as a term of respect.
_____ 7. "Grub-Wrangler" was cowboy slang for *cook*.
_____ 8. A cook's personality often had a great influence on the morale of the crew.
_____ 9. Each cowboy appreciated a little entertainment to liven up the lonely nights.
_____ 10. Cowboy coffee was usually brewed thick and black.

B. Now go back and correct the sentences above that you marked with a plus. Rewrite them on the back of this sheet, so they are true.

C. Compare the chuckwagon cook of the Old West with the chef of a modern gourmet restaurant. How are they alike? How do they differ?

D. For each word listed below, give the letter of the correct definition.

_____ 1. maxim   a. a benefit, a valuable addition
_____ 2. grueling   b. tender, emotional
_____ 3. moniker   c. difficult and exhausting
_____ 4. wrangler   d. requiring much work
_____ 5. arduous   e. an exciting story of questionable facts
_____ 6. asset   f. a saying
_____ 7. surrogate   g. bruised, bumped, or beaten
_____ 8. battered   h. a nickname
_____ 9. yarn   i. a substitute
_____ 10. sentimental   j. one who herds cattle

E. Use each vocabulary word above in an original sentence.

F. Use the characters below in a script for a TV western.
1. Slim, the hero
2. Shorty, his sidekick
3. Corkie, the cook
4. Miss Sallie, the school marm
5. Ma Miller and her sons, Clyde and Lester, the local cattle rustlers

Name _____

A Different Life

A woman quietly picked up a pen. "This is my letter to the world. . . " Bold words indeed, especially when you consider that their author refused to see strangers and spent most of her adult life within the confines of her own bedroom. Over 100 years later, people are still reading Emily Dickinson's letter to the world, along with 1,774 other poems she left behind. Both the woman and her work intrigue us, because neither follow well-trodden paths.

Emily Dickinson lived all her life in Amherst, Massachusetts, the daughter of a successful lawyer. Letters she wrote to her older brother describe the normal pranks and laughter of a happy childhood. At 17, along with other girls from Amherst, Emily enrolled in a college for young women. Here, scholars believe, a conflict took place that shaped the rest of Emily's life. The school required its students to conform to strict religious beliefs. Even though Emily was very shy, she already had her own well-developed ideas about God. The headmistress held daily meetings to convince Emily to change her mind, but she stubbornly refused.

After a year-long struggle, Emily withdrew from the college. She returned home to a quiet life with her parents, and her shyness intensified. She began to look to nature for wisdom and shaped her careful observations of backyard flowers and flies into odd verses packed with insight. The world of ideas began to consume her; events taking place outside her door faded in importance. One by one, the other young women of Amherst married, had children, and sent young men off to the Civil War, but Emily remained aloof from it all. By the time she was 30, she communicated with one or two friends and the next-door neighbors by letter only. When a visiting pianist offered to play, it was all Emily could do to listen from a hiding place in the hall. Yet the urge to write would overwhelm her; one year she averaged a poem a day for the entire year.

Despite her productivity, Emily never sought a large audience for her work. She shared just four or five poems with the few people she trusted: a neighbor, a sister-in-law, a literary critic with a well-known magazine. Those who saw the strange poems with their unconventional language and punctuation were most likely baffled; Emily's work met none of the standards by which poetry was then judged. It took more than 60 years for publishers to agree to print the poems exactly as Emily had written them.

And yet her work is timeless. It remains fresh and thoughtful despite ever-changing literary trends. One lone woman, limited in education and experience, armed only with observation and emotion, captured in words how it feels to be alive:

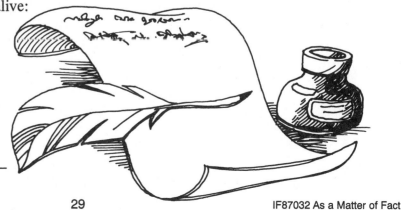

I taste a liquor never brewed—
From Tankards scooped in Pearl—
Not all the Frankfort Berries
Yield such an Alcohol!

Inebriate of Air—am I—
And Debauchee of Dew—
Reeling—thro endless summer days—
From inns of Molten Blue—

Name _____

A Different Life

A. Words are a poet's building blocks, and the right words make all the difference. On the back of this sheet, rewrite the two stanzas of Emily's poem from the end of the reading selection, replacing each creative word with a more common synonym or definition. What do ordinary words do to these verses?

B. Write T for true or F for false.
   _____ 1. There was no clue in Emily's early years that she would take a direction so different from most women of her day.
   _____ 2. Emily and her brother did not get along well together.
   _____ 3. Her college experience was a liberating one.
   _____ 4. Compromise was foreign to Emily.
   _____ 5. By the time she was 30, she had many close friends in the town of Amherst.
   _____ 6. The Civil War was a grave concern for Emily.
   _____ 7. Emily wrote her poems mainly for herself.
   _____ 8. The first people who read her poetry wanted to correct the odd punctuation.
   _____ 9. Emily drew inspiration for her poems mainly from the wide assortment of books she read.
   _____ 10. Her poetry provides many tidbits about day-to-day living in the 1860s—what ordinary people ate and wore, what they read and talked about.
   _____ 11. Emily stayed in her room because she was basically lazy.
   _____ 12. She learned more from observing nature than she did from attending school.

C. Were Emily's parents concerned about a daughter who lived her entire life hiding in the house? They probably were, but in those days, before psychology and psychiatry, more allowances were made for unusual people. How would modern parents handle a daughter like Emily? As Emily's mother or father, write a letter to Ann Landers, seeking advice about your daughter's talent and unusual lifestyle. Then write Ann's answer.

D. Predict a different outcome. What if Emily's parents had required her to
   1. stay in school, and
   2. live the normal life of a nineteenth-century woman? What do you think might have happened to Emily? Give at least three reasons for your opinion.

E. Read some of Emily's poems. Choose one to share out loud with the class. Be ready to say what you think the poem means and why you like it.

F. Draw or paint an illustration, write music, dance, or pantomime to the poem you selected above. Make the poet's words come to life in your artistic expression!

Name _____

A Voice for the Seas

He is considered the most famous ocean explorer of all time, and his underwater innovations have made the seas accessible to millions. But it was only an accident that opened Jacques Cousteau's eyes to the world beneath the waves.

As a young man growing up in France, Jacques had his eyes on the skies. He wanted to explore the clouds, and he trained to be a military pilot until an automobile wreck ended his career. Suffering debilitating injuries in both arms, Jacques began to swim daily to regain strength. After a few weeks of paddling around in the Mediterranean, he borrowed a pair of goggles and peered under the waves for the first time. With the return of his health came the familiar urge to explore. But now his focus was the ocean—to see and experience its wonders firsthand.

The problem, Jacques quickly learned, was with equipment. Heavy diving suits were cumbersome and the diver's only air supply was a hose to the surface. So Jacques and an engineer friend began to experiment. By 1943 they had developed a lightweight breathing apparatus that allowed the diver freedom of movement—scuba gear. The equipment gave people a wonderful new way to work and play in the sea.

Cousteau went on to conquer other technical challenges. He developed underwater cameras and submarines. His ship, the *Calypso*, became a floating lab for scientists studying water pollution. Right up until his death at age 87 in 1997, he worked to protect and promote the undersea world that captivated him for more than 50 years.

A. Predict a different outcome. Would Jacques Cousteau have been as famous or made as much difference in the world if he had become a pilot as he originally planned? Explain with reasons.

B. "The oceans are in danger of dying," Cousteau wrote in 1970. Choose one of the problems below to research.
   1. oil spills
   2. waste-dumping
   3. red tide
   4. ocean drilling
   5. ownership of oceans
   6. over-fishing

C. Haiku poetry packs much meaning and beauty into three short lines of five, seven, and five syllables:
   > Quiet waves leaving
   > bits of broken palaces
   > only children find

On a separate sheet of paper, write a haiku poem of your own in which you describe some aspect of the ocean. You may use one of the lines below for a starter or come up with your own.
   Red coral fingers
   Dolphin's back shining
   Startled blue tang darts

   Combed by mermaid's hand
   Silent world waiting
   Barracuda lurks

Name _____

24 Hours of Power

The people of tiny Frogtown were so proud! One of their own boys had made it, all the way to the White House. His name was David Rice Atchison and, legally, he was president of the United States for one whole day.

Atchison was serving as the leader of the U.S. Senate on March 4, 1849, the day Zachary Taylor was scheduled to succeed James K. Polk as the country's twelfth president. Taylor was a man of deep faith who lived out his convictions. Because March 4 fell on a Sunday, Taylor wanted to wait until Monday, March 5 for his swearing-in ceremony. The delay meant that, technically, the country would be without a duly elected chief executive for 24 hours. Under American law, should both the president and vice-president be unable to serve, the third in line would be the leader of the Senate: David Rice Atchison. He decided to relish his single day of power. Setting out a feast, he invited all his friends to an evening of revelry, during which he commissioned each of them to a post of power—for one day only. By noon the next day, Zachary Taylor took over, ending the country's shortest and merriest presidency.

David Rice Atchison returned to his post in the U.S. Senate. After serving his country there, he retired from public life and slipped silently into the pages of historical trivia.

A. Circle the best title for the selection.
   1. The One-Day Wonder
   2. The Life of David Rice Atchison
   3. The President's Stand-In
   4. Presidential Party
   5. The Senator Who Became President

B. Answer these vocabulary questions on the back of this sheet.
   1. What are your *convictions* concerning capital punishment?
   2. Give your own recipe for *revelry.*
   3. Share some *trivia* that is lodged in your brain.
   4. What meal do you *relish* most after a day of hard exercise?
   5. To what family jobs have you been *commissioned*? Explain.

C. What happened first? Number the sentences in chronological order, from 1 to 8.
   _____ 1. Taylor schedules oath of office for Monday.
   _____ 2. Atchison elected to U.S. Senate.
   _____ 3. Atchison retires to obscurity.
   _____ 4. Atchison born in Frogtown, Kentucky.
   _____ 5. Taylor elected president.
   _____ 6. Taylor takes oath as president.
   _____ 7. Atchison resumes leadership of Senate.
   _____ 8. Atchison takes office for 24 hours.

Name _____

Baby Island Baby Sitter

Arne Jonsson had a most unconventional job, babysitting a brand-new island. Surtsey was born on November 14, 1963, when a volcano erupted in the North Atlantic Ocean near Iceland. After months of steaming and exploding, a tiny island, complete with lava cliffs and black sand beaches, stood where only waves had washed before. People curious about the newest place on earth rushed to Surtsey's shore. That is when scientists realized that the baby island needed protection. Surtsey offered a once-in-a-lifetime opportunity to study the processes that long ago had filled our planet with plants and animals. If Surtsey was going to grow and develop so that it would have its own life forms, it needed a baby sitter, someone who would make certain the tiny island was not disturbed.

The scientists hired Arne Jonsson and built him a miniscule hut on Surtsey, just big enough for one bed and a table. Mr. Jonsson moved in while parts of the island were still smoking from hot lava flows. Every night, the ground shook. But Jonsson loved the excitement of watching Surtsey grow larger and larger. It made up for living all alone in the lap of a volcano!

Mr. Jonsson turned all visitors away from his island's shore except for scientists who came to perform vital tests and take measurements. Even with these guests, the island baby sitter was extremely strict. There could be no seeds or bits of dirt from the mainland hiding in pockets or pant legs. Eating was allowed only inside the hut, for one scrap of apple dropped on the ground could modify the pattern of life developing on Surtsey. When the scientists left, they carried off every bit of trash they had created.

Mr. Jonsson was there when birds stopped to rest on the island, depositing the first seeds. He found the very first green shoots of plant growth and watched the first nest being built on the cliffs. Two and half years after Surtsey's emergence from the ocean as a volcanic dome, the first tiny white flower bloomed. It yielded six seeds. Slowly but surely, life was taking hold. What had happened all over the planet many years ago was happening once more on tiny Surtsey.

Today, smoke still curls from Surtsey's craters, and scientists continue to watch the island develop. Mr. Jonsson's days there are over, but guess what kind of baby pictures he loves to display in his home on the mainland!

Name _____

Baby Island Baby Sitter ━━━━━━━━━━━━━▼

A. For each word write the letter of the correct definition.

_____	1. unconventional	a.	the act of coming into view
_____	2. miniscule	b.	very tiny
_____	3. modify	c.	to produce; bear
_____	4. emergence	d.	out of the ordinary
_____	5. yield	e.	alter, change

B. On the back of this sheet, answer these vocabulary questions.
1. How can a person *modify* his or her hairstyle?
2. What will be the date of your *emergence* onto the high school scene?
3. What has hard work *yielded* for you this school year?
4. Describe an item of clothing in your closet that is *unconventional*. Explain.
5. Many folk tales and children's stories feature characters who are *miniscule*. List as many as you can.

C. Make up an acrostic about the new island. Write a descriptive word or phrase beginning with each letter.

S =
U =
R =
T =
S =
E =
Y =

D. Think and answer.
1. Explain how a single apple could change life on Surtsey.
2. List at least five character traits helpful for someone interested in becoming an island baby sitter. Give reasons for each trait.
3. The ancient Icelandic god of fire was Surtur. Explain the connection with the new island.
4. Few people are permitted to visit Surtsey. If given the opportunity, would you go? Why or why not?

E. What happened first? Number the events from 1 to 8 in chronological order.
_____ 1. A hut is built.
_____ 2. Curiosity-seekers walk all over the new island.
_____ 3. All trash is carried off Surtsey.
_____ 4. An island forms from the lava.
_____ 5. Scientists are concerned the visitors will pollute the new island.
_____ 6. A volcano erupts in the ocean near Iceland.
_____ 7. Visitors' pockets and pants are checked.
_____ 8. Mr. Jonsson is hired.

Name _____

King of "Mosts" ➤

"The Most Wealth, the Most Women, the Most Wisdom"—the headline could describe any one of several men in today's business and entertainment news. But the individual who best typifies these superlatives leaps larger than life from the pages of ancient history, King Solomon of Israel.

Solomon's reign of unparalleled privilege began in 965 B.C. with his quest for wisdom. According to scripture, Solomon prayed for the ability to judge wisely. God granted this request. The young king became an expert in botany, zoology, government administration, and architecture. He wrote over 4,000 sage sayings and songs. Soon rulers from other nations sought—and paid—for Solomon's counsel. The Queen of Sheba alone gave him over three million dollars' worth of gold, along with large quantities of rare spices, in appreciation for his help. But great wealth must have clouded Solomon's mind, for he developed in his mature years an obsession that led to his downfall: women. Solomon officially married 700 wives and brought another 300 to live in the palace. With the king's focus so diverted, cracks began to form and the once-great nation of Israel splintered after his death.

A. For each word write the letter of the correct definition.

_____ 1. typify   a. wise
_____ 2. superlative   b. to turn aside
_____ 3. unparalleled   c. an inescapable preoccupation
_____ 4. botany   d. the highest degree of something
_____ 5. zoology   e. the study of plants
_____ 6. sage   f. to represent, to have the main characteristics of something
_____ 7. counsel   g. advice
_____ 8. obsession   h. the study of animals
_____ 9. divert   i. having no equal

B. On a sheet of notebook paper, write an original sentence for each word listed above.

C. Think and write.
1. What world record would you like to hold? Why? What responsibilities would come with the title?
2. Plan a way to set a classroom record. Submit your plan in writing and, as a class, choose three to actually attempt.
3. Solomon's life crumbled in his later years. What time of life do you believe to be the most difficult? Give at least three reasons for your answer.

D. You learned the meaning of *zoology* in exercise A. List and define as many other "ologies" as you can. Here are some starters. Use another sheet of paper if you need to.
1. astrology   4. audiology
2. cardiology   5. seismology
3. dermatology   6. ichthyology

Name _____

Dr. Seuss on the Loose

The Obsk, the Oobleck, Greeches, Grinches, Sneetches, Barba-Loots, and Sam-I-Am—what wonderful characters we would have missed if Theodor Seuss Geisel had not been a persistent man. While on a turbulent ocean voyage in 1937, the young artist began doodling to keep his mind off his queasy stomach. A simple, rhyming story with a preposterous plot began to take shape. Twenty-eight companies rejected Geisel's manuscript. It was too different, they claimed, from other children's books on the market. But the twenty-ninth publisher took a chance, and glorious characters have found a home in our hearts ever since.

Most adults considered Theodor Geisel an amusing eccentric, a college dropout who signed silly drawings with an assumed title and his middle name. But children recognized at once a genius with a twinkle in his eye, an adult who had not forgotten how to fantasize, who could pull the primmest teacher into his world of rhyme and romp. For the first time, books that helped kids learn to read were actually fun. Many a voracious reader can point to a Seuss title as the start of a lifelong avocation: *Horton Hears a Who, McElligot's Pool, The Cat in the Hat, Hop on Pop, Green Eggs and Ham.*

Theodor Geisel went on to write and illustrate 42 books' worth of his particular brand of magic. He died in 1991 at age 87, but every time a budding reader chooses one of his books off the shelf, Dr. Seuss lives again, forever young, forever fun.

A.   According to an old saying, "Imitation is the sincerest form of flattery." Reread your favorite Dr. Seuss book and then write your own version, complete with wacky rhymes and pictures, on another sheet of paper.

B.   For each vocabulary word below, choose the correct synonyms. (There may be more than one for each word.)

1. turbulent: a) lengthy   b) stormy   c) rough   d) boring
2. queasy: a) nauseated   b) empty   c) rumbling   d) oily
3. eccentric: a) circular   b) clown   c) oddball   d) grouch
4. primmest: a) dullest   b) strictest   c) most formal   d) stiffest
5. voracious: a) eager   b) hungry   c) slow   d) immature
6. avocation: a) occupation   b) hobby   c) job   d) preoccupation

C.   Theodor Geisel spent much effort finding a publisher for a book that some considered silly and worthless. "Put your efforts into things that will count," they said. Explain the chain of consequences that would have occurred if Dr. Seuss had listened to his critics. How can someone know when to persist and when to quit? What does our persistence do for us? For others? Write your thoughts on the back of this sheet.

Name _____

Final Flight ◀▽

The journey was supposed to be her last. One final, exhilarating, record-breaking flight and Amelia Earhart planned to settle down. The year was 1937, and America's premiere aviatrix and her navigator were flying toward tiny Howland Island in the Pacific Ocean, on the longest leg of their flight. If successful, Amelia would be the first pilot, male or female, to circle the globe at the equator. It was an era marked by hero-worship, and Americans admired Amelia for her pioneering accomplishments in aviation. More than that, they loved her charming, tom-boy ways. She was America's sweetheart, kid sister, and girl next door all rolled into one, with an infectious grin that lit up the skies.

But Amelia never made it to Howland. Somewhere over the Pacific, her plane just disappeared. The nation held its breath as searchers combed the area for clues. George Putnam, Amelia's husband, painstakingly tracked down every lead, legitimate or absurd, for more than a year. But no trace of Amelia, navigator Fred Noonan, or the plane was ever found. Despite the evidence—or lack of it—no one wanted to believe she was gone. Perhaps that is why the rumors began, stories that continue to make headlines to this very day. Each scrap of rusted metal that washes ashore in the Central Pacific renews interest in the unsolved mystery. Some theories have Amelia on a secret mission for the government; others claim her plane was forced down on a Japanese-occupied island. Some hypothesize that she secretly returned to the United States and assumed a new identity in order to escape the crowds that continually mobbed her.

But most experts construct a far less dramatic scenario. They believe that Amelia simply ran out of gas, searching for an island that was not where it was supposed to be. The best navigational charts available in those days placed Howland Island a few degrees from its actual location. Just as any other lost pilot would do, Amelia and her navigator probably flew a search pattern looking for Howland until their plane went down and crashed in the sea. More than 60 years have passed, but the courageous spirit Amelia showed lives on in each record that is broken, in every barrier that is overcome. She flew to beat the odds, smiling all the way, and showed the world some of what it means to be an American.

Final Flight ——————————————————————— ▼

Name _____

A. Match these vocabulary riddles with the correct answers.

_____ 1. an infectious skin allergy is . . . .   a. a higher flyer

_____ 2. an exhilarating dental procedure is . . . .   b. a real deal

_____ 3. loftier aviatrix is . . . .   c. thrilling drilling

_____ 4. a legitimate bargain is . . . .   d. the premiere buccaneer

_____ 5. to suggest plenty of excuses is . . . .   e. to hypothesize alibis

_____ 6. the most outstanding among pirates is . . . .   f. scratching that's catching

B. Research one of these famous females.
1. Mary McLeod Bethune   2. Susan B. Anthony
3. Nellie Tayloe Ross   4. Elizabeth Pinckney
5. Althea Gibson   6. Sarah Bernhardt

C. Circle the best title for the selection.
1. First Female of Flight
2. Flight into Mystery
3. Amelia's Smile
4. The Missing Island

D. Think and write.
1. Discuss "Amelia Appeal." Why do Americans continue to be fascinated by a young woman who disappeared over 60 years ago? What if Amelia had made it home and settled down to a normal life?
2. If Amelia had made it to a desert island, she might have tried to send a message home in a bottle. What would her message have said? Write her final letter to the world.

E. What happened first? Number the events from 1 to 6 in chronological order.

_____ 1. Amelia never makes it to Howland.

_____ 2. Theories still discussed 60 years later.

_____ 3. Amelia decides to set world record for transglobal flight.

_____ 4. Amelia's disappearance mourned by American public.

_____ 5. Amelia loved by American public for her accomplishments and personality.

_____ 6. Amelia last heard from heading toward Howland Island in the Pacific Ocean.

F. Amelia once said, "Everyone has his own oceans to fly." What is your great ocean in life? Share your dream in the form of a poem, a drawing, a song, a dance, a skit, or an essay.

Name _____

The Collector-Collector ⟶ ▼

Look over the names that identify the members of the animal kingdom, and you will find one repeated over and over again. There is a Baird's octopus, a Baird's dolphin, a Baird's sparrow, a Baird's sandpiper, and a Baird's tapir, just to name a few. More than 40 species of animals are named for Spencer Fullerton Baird, the "collector-collector" of the Smithsonian's Museum of Natural History in Washington, D.C.

Baird was hired in 1850, shortly after Congress established the Smithsonian. His job was to assemble collections of birds, animals, insects, fish, plants, and rocks to provide an accurate picture of life on earth—a gargantuan task! But the 27-year-old had a headstart—two railroad boxcars overflowing with bones, skins, feathers, and eggs he had collected himself since childhood. From long days spent in the woods, Baird knew the best way to press plants and pickle animal skins, where to look for rare insects, and how to ship fragile egg specimens by wagon train. And he knew the people best acquainted with America's wildlife; John James Audubon, the famed painter of birds, had himself written the recommendation that secured Baird the museum post.

The new museum, Baird realized, would need much more than he could ever collect on his own, so he called on these wildlife experts: fur trappers, remote lighthouse keepers, army doctors, missionaries to faraway lands—anyone who would ship beetles or birds' nests back to Washington became part of the network. While he could not pay his people in the field, Baird kept them stocked with the hard-to-find supplies collectors need: alcohol for preserving samples, insect pins and mounting board, fish-collecting trunks, lures, and ammunition. He also wrote encouraging letters full of news from home, a rare treat in those days for people stationed at the ends of the earth. Because of Baird's own enthusiasm and commitment, a small army of collectors caught the vision for a museum that would study and display the wonders of the natural world.

Many of these collectors served Baird loyally for years and often named the new species they found in his honor. Much to his sorrow, Baird himself never got back to the field to collect again. There simply was not time. But because he worked at collecting collectors, America's Museum of Natural History became one of the finest in the world.

Name _____

The Collector-Collector

A. What makes a good collector? List three important character traits. What makes a good "behind-the-scenes" person like Spencer Fullerton Baird? Give three traits. How was it important that Baird had been a collector himself? Write your answers on the back of this sheet.

B. Explain the meaning of this statement: "A museum exists in three different time zones. It serves memory and time past, it sheds light on the present, and it points the way to possibilities for the future."

C. Plan a museum of your own. What would you collect and why? How would you go about securing specimens to display?

D. For each quotation, give the correct speaker.
   1. "My son's pockets are always full of frogs and bark and snake skins. He still acts like a little boy, playing all day in the woods. Won't he ever settle down and get a decent job?"
      _____
   2. "Wow, the sign says that the great auk became extinct more than 150 years ago, after auk-feather hats became stylish. Just look at that funny beak!" _____
   3. "A letter from the States! And some new fish nets! Bless that man! If it weren't for him, I might go crazy out here." _____
   4. "What has Jones found now? His packages just take my breath away!"_____

E. The word *gargantuan* comes from a character in a book, a giant named Gargantua. We commonly use well-known literary characters to pack our writing with more meaning. Fill in each blank below with the correct literary name.

Jack and Jill	Gulliver	Cinderella	Sleeping Beauty	Noah
Thumbelina	Pinocchio	Peter Pan	Goliath	Humpty Dumpty

1. Uncle John was the _____ of our family; he never outgrew playing silly tricks and games.
2. We love a _____ story, where a rich young man falls in love with a sweet poor girl.
3. Like _____, his big, round, grinning face cracked into a million pieces when he heard the bad news.
4. "Don't pull a _____ on me, young man. I will know if you are telling the truth."
5. Meeting his Japanese hosts, the American football player felt like _____ among the Lilliputians.
6. We call my grandmother Mrs. _____ because of all her pets.
7. For many years, China was a _____, but she is awakening to her role in world politics at last.

Name _____

A Foot in Two Worlds

"Playful One" was Wahunsonacook's favorite daughter. Hers should have been a life of privilege, married to a leading warrior of her tribe. But the day Pocahontas knelt to shield John Smith's head from a war club, her life changed forever. Romantics have spun a love story between the English settler and the Powhatan girl, but the facts show much more— two cultures on a collision course, held off for a short time by one young woman.

When the English landed in Virginia, they did not know how to survive. Wahunsonacook's people supplied food. They taught the colonists to grow corn and tobacco. But the settlers' greed for land worried the chief. In a ceremony of which Captain Smith understood little, the chief adopted him into the Powhatan tribe. The staging of an execution and the rescue by Pocahontas symbolized that Smith's old life was over. In adopting Smith, Wahunsonacook hoped the white settlers would choose to follow tribal ways of life. An uneasy peace reigned for a time.

Then Pocahontas married a young English settler, John Rolfe. She traveled to England with him to raise funds for the struggling colony. Her son Thomas was born there. Meanwhile, settlers continued to grab land. Her father ordered them killed and their mouths stuffed with dirt as a warning against greed. Pocahontas planned to return home, to stop the violence from escalating. Waiting for the ship that would return her to America, Pocahontas contracted smallpox and died.

A. On the back of this sheet, write a concluding sentence for this selection. Make certain that it restates the main point of the introduction.

B. Pocahontas' son, Thomas Rolfe, was raised in England but returned to Virginia as a young man. Write a story as Thomas, describing his feelings when he sees his mother's homeland for the first time.

C. Many Native-American words enrich the English language today. Do one of the following on the back of this sheet.
1. Using maps and reference books, list places bearing Indian names. There are hundreds; try for at least 25.
2. Use each of these Native-American words in an original sentence: *chamois, succotash, quinine, chinquapin, caribou, tattoo, travois, jerky, guava, alpaca, pampas.*

D. The selection above omits many events in the life of Pocahontas. Research to answer these questions:
1. Who married Pocahontas before John Rolfe did?
2. Who kept Pocahontas as a prisoner on a ship?
3. What was her English name?
4. What did people in England think of Pocahontas?

Name _____

Comic Book Code Breaker

"Get your nose out of that comic book!" parents like to say. But reading comics really paid off for David Stuart, the youngest, most successful interpreter of ancient Mayan hieroglyphics.

The Mayans were a highly advanced people who built great cities on the Yucatán Peninsula of Central America from A.D. 250 to 900. Sophisticated astronomers and mathematicians, they left behind many stone tablets and monuments covered with picture-writing. Each one could give us valuable information about the Mayans, but the symbols they used were almost impossible to interpret. David Stuart was only 11 years old when he took a look at an ancient tablet that had stumped scientists for more than five years. The hands, faces, and action figures carved in stone reminded him of his comic books. The more David looked, the more fascinated he became and, after eight hours, he had figured out the message of the tablet.

The scientists were amazed. They gave David more hieroglyphics to interpret. By age 18, he had translated more Mayan tablets than any other expert had ever done. He earned a large cash prize for his work advancing our knowledge of the Mayan people. With the money, he traveled to Central America to see the ancient cities firsthand, and he bought a computer to help keep track of the hundreds of symbols he had translated. Today, David teaches at Harvard University, and he still thinks cracking a Mayan picture code is as much fun as reading a modern action comic book!

A. Write T for true or F for false.
   _____ 1. The Mayans were building their cities around the time of Christ.
   _____ 2. David Stuart had read many comic books before translating his first Mayan tablet.
   _____ 3. David got little recognition for his work.
   _____ 4. His many childhood visits to Mayan cities gave David an advantage when he made his first translation.
   _____ 5. The Mayan hieroglyphics are a series of lines, circles, and squiggles.

B. An alternate title for this selection could be "Through the Eyes of a Child." Explain why David's age may have been an advantage.

C. Complete one of these activities.
   1. Create a comic book version of David Stuart's story.
   2. Create your own hieroglyphic code. Write a message and challenge your classmates to translate it.

D. Research to learn more about the Mayan civilization.

Name _____

Mary's Madness ➤

What started with a simple trip to the shore in 1804 became a lifelong passion that made a young girl's name known to scientists all over the world.

Mary Anning lived with her family on the English coast, in the small resort village of Lyme Regis. When Mary turned five, she and her father began hiking together along the blue slate cliffs that ran beside the shore. They often found rocks imprinted with strange-looking seashells, unlike any of those that would wash up in the waves. Mary's father collected the odd rocks to sell to summer tourists for souvenirs. (In those days, the term *fossil* was not commonly understood.) When Mary's father died, the ten-year-old continued their habit on her own. Almost every day, she could be seen combing the cliffs, head down, eyes peeled for curiosities. The people of Lyme Regis gently joked about young Mary's "madness."

One day, however, two years later, their laughter turned to gasps of amazement. Breathless and wide-eyed, Mary dragged some men from the village out to the beach. She pointed to a layer in the cliffs. There, preserved in the rock, was the seven-foot skeleton of a creature no one had ever seen before. It had the head of a dolphin, the chest of a lizard, the fins of a whale, and the backbone of a fish. The villagers helped the young girl dig the chunk of fossilized bones out of the cliff. A wealthy nobleman who lived nearby purchased the heavy stone from Mary, paying over $100 for it, a substantial sum in those days. He shipped the rock to a museum where scientists rushed to examine the amazing find. They christened the strange creature *ichthyosaur*, or fish-lizard, and asked Mary to look for more of the petrified bones.

Mary spent the rest of her life studying her precious cliffs. She learned which layers of rock would reveal the secrets of the prehistoric past. Soon she stumbled on her second great skeleton, a plesiosaur. Museums and universities all over the world placed orders for fossils to study. A king visiting England made a trip to her shop in Lyme Regis, to view her collection of bones preserved in stone and to purchase some for himself. Shortly before Mary died, she made a third incredible discovery, the skeleton of a pterosaur, the first ever found in Britain.

Thanks to Mary Anning, scientists began the patient work of reading the stories told by ancient bones, work that continues to this day as the study of paleontology. And Mary herself is not forgotten. If you visit the church in Lyme Regis, you will see a stained glass window that commemorates her pioneering efforts.

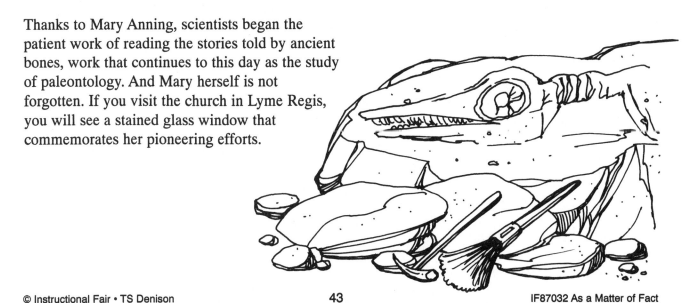

Name _____

Mary's Madness

A. Be creative! Choose one of the ways below to tell the story of Mary Anning.
    1. Design your own version of the stained glass window that shows Mary and her bones. Make certain any fossils you include are accurate.
    2. Create the front page of the London newspaper that announced Mary's first find. Report on various opinions about the bones—from scholars, to shopkeepers, to children, to King George III.

B. As a class, come up with at least ten personality traits of a good fossil-hunter. Discuss reasons for each trait.

C. Mary discovered her first skeleton in 1811, launching the new science of paleontology. What else was happening around the world during the year 1811? Include events from Great Britain, the United States, France, China, Japan, and Africa. Write your answers on another sheet of paper.

D. With Mary's first skeleton, scientists began the system still used today of giving fossils names based on Latin or Greek words. Use a dictionary to find the meaning of each dinosaur name below.

    1. allosaurus   _____
    2. brachiosaurus   _____
    3. diplodocus   _____
    4. camptosaurus   _____
    5. stegosaurus   _____
    6. trachodon   _____
    7. ankylosaurus   _____
    8. protoceratops   _____
    9. triceratops   _____
    10. iguanodon   _____
    11. tyrannosaurus rex _____
    12. plesiosaurus   _____
    13. pteranodon   _____
    14. archaeopteryx   _____

E. Write T for true or F for false.

    _____ 1. The people of Lyme Regis came to appreciate Mary's "madness."

    _____ 2. Mary's father found the first evidence of prehistoric life washing up in the waves off Lyme Regis.

    _____ 3. Mary traveled all over England, looking for more fossilized skeletons.

    _____ 4. Even though she had little formal education, by the end of her life, Mary knew as much about finding fossils in the slate cliffs of the English shore as any other scientist in Britain.

    _____ 5. Mary made enough money on the fossils she sold to care for her family.

    _____ 6. Wealthy people in Mary's day showed little interest in scientific discoveries.

    _____ 7. Besides the three skeletons Mary discovered, the cliffs around Lyme Regis yielded few other bones.

    _____ 8. Before Mary's discoveries, the only visitors to Lyme Regis had been summer vacationers.

Name _____

The Will to Run

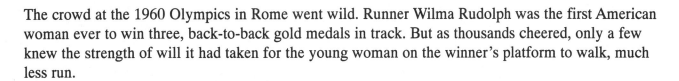

The crowd at the 1960 Olympics in Rome went wild. Runner Wilma Rudolph was the first American woman ever to win three, back-to-back gold medals in track. But as thousands cheered, only a few knew the strength of will it had taken for the young woman on the winner's platform to walk, much less run.

Wilma was the seventeenth child of an African-American family in Clarksville, Tennessee. Sickly and underweight at birth, she had just learned to walk at age four when she became dangerously ill. For weeks, the family watched their little girl struggle for her life. The illness finally passed but left Wilma's left leg paralyzed. Doctors advised her mother there was only a remote chance the child would ever walk unaided. Mrs. Rudolph marched home and set up a strict family schedule; she and the older children would massage Wilma's leg four times a day every day. They would not stop until their sister was strong and healthy. Family members rubbed and kneaded the weak little leg every night long after Wilma had fallen asleep.

Two years later, Wilma managed to hop for short distances. By the time she was eight, she was dragging a leg brace around and tossing a basketball into the peach basket her brothers had nailed up. When everyone else had to quit for the night, Wilma's mother let her determined daughter play a little longer, so she could catch up. The brace came off, and, by the time she was in high school, Wilma could run as well as any other girl—often better. She played on her school's basketball team and went out for track. The coach of Tennessee State's famous track team, the Tigerbelles, saw Wilma run. He saw legs that had grown long and powerful and, more importantly, he saw the will to run. If she would train hard, the coach told her, she had a good chance at a college scholarship and a spot with the Tigerbelles.

Wilma made it to Tennessee State, the first of her brothers and sisters to go to college. To her family, she was a star, but old memories of the crippled leg worried Wilma. Could she really compete on a college level? Her mother came to the rescue again. "Don't think about the past. Just concentrate on trying hard now."

Soon, Wilma and three teammates became one of the fastest relay squads in the country. Scheduled to attend Olympic try-outs, they were training hard when Wilma's times suddenly started to slip. Extra practice, adjustments in technique—nothing seemed to help. The coach finally took Wilma to a doctor. Almost immediately, the source of the trouble was spotted—infected tonsils that had drained her strength for years! Three weeks after the tonsils came out, Wilma set new world records at the Olympic trials, followed by gold-medal times in Rome. The victory was a testament to the power of determination—her family's, her coach's, and most of all, her own.

Name _____

The Will to Run ▼

A. Every step of the way to the Olympics, there were people who thought Wilma would never make it. For each quotation below, identify the time in Wilma's life.

_____ 1. "Just who does she think she is? None of the other Rudolph children tried to go."

_____ 2. "This puny little one will never make it. She has 16 in line in front of her!"

_____ 3. "Well, that's the end of our dream, girls, unless we go find another runner for the squad. She'll need at least six weeks to recover."

_____ 4. "It's great she can get around, but she'll probably need that thing the rest of her life."

_____ 5. "Poor child—just learned to walk, and now this! Even if she survives, what chance for a normal healthy life will she have?"

B. Think and answer.

1. A famous coach once said, "No athlete wins on his or her own. Each and every victory requires the backing of a team." Explain how this statement applied to Wilma Rudolph.

2. Tell how an obstacle or problem can often turn out to be a blessing in disguise. Include examples from Wilma's life.

3. Wilma's mother told her to forget the past and just concentrate on the present. Tell about a time you had to do that in order to succeed.

4. For many gold medalists, life after the Olympics is tough. They miss the spotlight. From what you have read, predict what Wilma's life was like following the Olympics.

C. Learn more about one of these famous Olympians.

1. Jesse Owens   2. Jim Thorpe
3. Babe Zaharias   4. Johnny Weissmuller
5. Sonja Henie   6. Esther Williams

D. Each of the people below overcame physical challenges to make important contributions to society. Write the letter of the correct name beside each description.

a. Helen Keller   f. John Milton
b. Franklin D. Roosevelt   g. Stevie Wonder
c. Louis Braille   h. Thomas Edison
d. Ludwig van Beethoven   i. Henri de Toulouse-Lautrec
e. Fanny Crosby   j. Francisco Goya

_____ 1. German composer, wrote greatest music after he became deaf.

_____ 2. English poet, became blind before he wrote his great masterpiece, *Paradise Lost*.

_____ 3. Paralyzed in both legs by polio, became president of the United States.

_____ 4. Blind from childhood, she wrote many beloved hymns.

_____ 5. Blind and deaf from childhood, she became a spokesperson for people with disabilities.

_____ 6. A composer and performer of popular music, blind almost from birth.

_____ 7. An injury left the greatest inventor in history hard of hearing.

_____ 8. One of the first masters of modern art lost his hearing during an illness.

_____ 9. This blind teacher developed a system of writing and printing for the blind.

_____ 10. An injury stunted the growth of this French painter.

Name _____

Polar Friendship

Robert Peary was world-famous for his expeditions into uncharted Arctic regions. As he prepared for his final attempt to reach the north pole in 1908, skilled adventurers around the world petitioned Peary for the privilege of accompanying him. Of all the people he could have selected, he insisted on the one man he trusted with his very life, African-American Matthew Henson.

An inseparable pair, the two were from very different backgrounds. Peary, a white, college-educated, family man, had seven years of government service under his belt, surveying the jungles of Nicaragua. Matthew Henson was a 24-year-old fresh off his family's Maryland farm, whose only discernible skill was in handling dogs. The two worked together for the first time in 1891, when Peary set out with a team to explore the icecap of Greenland. Although the expedition included several men experienced in polar exploration, it was Henson in particular who impressed Robert Peary.

In addition to keeping their team of sled dogs fit, Henson demonstrated a unique ability to communicate with the native people they encountered. Intrigued by Henson's dark face, the Eskimos taught him the skills that helped his team survive in the frozen north. Previous Arctic explorers had burdened themselves with masses of supplies, only to become stranded and freeze to death. At Henson's urging, Peary jettisoned their heavy American equipment for Eskimo-style clothing, sleds, tools, and food. It was the key to their success.

With Greenland properly charted, Peary was ready to locate the north pole. He and Henson sailed north in a ship equipped to withstand razor-sharp floes, but difficulties forced them to turn back 200 miles short of reaching their goal. At age 52, Peary knew he probably only had the health and strength for one last try.

So in 1908 he and Matthew Henson gathered a large group of Eskimo and white men, along with over 100 dogs, for a final assault. They traveled as a large group until they drew within 140 miles of the pole. That's when Peary, Henson, and four Eskimos journeyed on alone. Crossing ice that crumbled behind them, stumbling mile after mile on feet too numb to feel, they stopped roughly three miles from the pole on April 6, 1909. Lacking precise instruments, they crisscrossed the entire area, just to make certain they came as close as possible to the actual spot. Matthew Henson returned home a hero for his role in reaching the north pole. In an era that offered his race little opportunity or recognition, Henson proved that friendship, ability, and hard work could thaw frozen barriers, at home and in the far north.

Polar Friendship

Name _____

A. For each word write the letter of the correct definition.

_____	1. petition	a.	a mass of floating ice
_____	2. inseparable	b.	fascinated
_____	3. surveyor	c.	to make a request, to plead for
_____	4. discernible	d.	weighed down
_____	5. intrigued	e.	exactly defined
_____	6. burdened	f.	incapable of being disjoined
_____	7. jettison	g.	noticeable, apparent
_____	8. floe	h.	to throw overboard, to discard
_____	9. assault	i.	one who measures and charts land
_____	10. precise	j.	the final stage of an attack

B. On the back of this sheet, write an original sentence for each word listed above.

C. Code each clue below H for Henson or P for Peary.
   _____ 1. Had little formal education.
   _____ 2. Worked in both tropical and polar regions.
   _____ 3. Looked beyond external appearances to appreciate the character of a man.
   _____ 4. Convinced his team to eliminate heavy equipment.
   _____ 5. The older of the two men.
   _____ 6. Drew curious native people by his appearance and friendly manner.
   _____ 7. Animals thrived in his care.
   _____ 8. Bombarded by requests to join the polar team.

D. Others have made famous trips to the Arctic. Choose one of the topics below to research.
   1. Richard E. Byrd   5. USS *Nautilus*
   2. Floyd Bennett   6. Naomi Uemura
   3. Sir John Franklin   7. Roald Amundsen
   4. William Baffin   8. Henry Hudson

E. After they returned home, both Henson and Peary wrote books about their polar adventures. To help their readers experience the sights, sounds, smells, and feelings of the Arctic, they used similes and metaphors:
   The cold cut through my boots like a jagged knife.
   The midnight sun was a gloomy orange ball low in the sky.

   For each Arctic detail below, write your own simile or metaphor on the back of this sheet.
   1. the northern lights   6. sunrise on snow
   2. the quietness   7. sled dogs
   3. polar bears   8. the shape of icebergs
   4. walruses   9. a sea of floes
   5. whales   10. brilliant sun on ice

Name _____

War Host

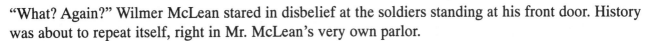

"What? Again?" Wilmer McLean stared in disbelief at the soldiers standing at his front door. History was about to repeat itself, right in Mr. McLean's very own parlor.

In 1861 Wilmer McLean was the owner of a prosperous grocery business in the Virginia town of Bull Run, also known as Manassas, not far from Washington, D.C. He lived with his family in a home well-suited to a man of his standing in the community. As a proud homeowner and a loyal son of Virginia, Mr. McLean was honored when General P.G.T. Beauregard of the newly formed Confederate Army asked to use the house as a temporary headquarters, to prepare for the first major land battle of the war. Mr. McLean, along

with most other Southerners, thought a grand battle or two would put a quick end to the debate over slavery. The McLean family was excited to have a front row seat as thousands of troops from both sides converged in the fields around their house. It was not long, however, before the McLeans changed their minds. A Yankee cannonball crashed into the house, completely destroying the kitchen, and the end of the day found the family desperately trying to help some of the 5,000 men dying just outside their door.

One year later, when fierce fighting returned to Bull Run, Mr. McLean had had enough. He moved his family to a place he thought the war would never reach, the tiny town called Appomattox Court House. But by an odd twist of fate, it was the McLeans' home once again that was chosen for one of the most important meetings of the war. In Wilmer McLean's front parlor, Robert E. Lee surrendered the Confederate forces to Union commander Ulysses S. Grant on April 9, 1865. Mr. McLean would go down in history as the man in whose house the Civil War began and ended.

A. Select the saying that best expresses the truth of this selection and explain.
   1. A man is known by the company he keeps.
   2. Forewarned is forearmed.
   3. Truth is often stranger than fiction.
   4. War makes strange bedfellows.
   5. He who fights and runs away, lives to fight another day.

B. More Civil War battles were fought in Virginia than in any other state. Trace a map of Virginia and locate the battlefields listed below. Explain why Appomattox Court House appeared to be a safe place for the McLean family when they moved in 1862.

Bull Run (Manassas)	Fredericksburg
Cold Harbor	Spotsylvania Court House
Chancellorsville	Wilderness
Hampton Roads	Fair Oaks
Petersburg	

Name _____

Vegetable Inventor ➤

Lennie loved digging in dirt when he was a boy. He would bury odd objects just to see what different kinds of plants he could get to grow.

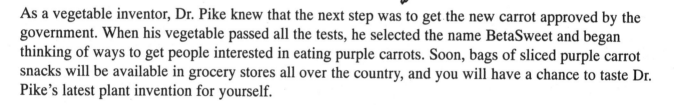

Dr. Leonard Pike is an adult now, but he still loves to experiment with plants in his laboratory at Texas A & M University. Dr. Pike is a vegetable inventor. Using chemicals, he takes information from one plant's cells to mix with another plant. This is called gene-splicing, and the results often yield bizarre-looking plants. Take the case of the purple carrots. When Dr. Pike found some reddish carrots growing in his test gardens, he began mixing their genes together. After several growing seasons, he had carrots that went from purple on the outside to orange-yellow on the inside. As unusual as these carrots looked, he discovered that they were extra sweet and delicious. When he tested the nutrient levels, he found the purple carrots were very high in beta-carotene, a cancer-fighting agent.

As a vegetable inventor, Dr. Pike knew that the next step was to get the new carrot approved by the government. When his vegetable passed all the tests, he selected the name BetaSweet and began thinking of ways to get people interested in eating purple carrots. Soon, bags of sliced purple carrot snacks will be available in grocery stores all over the country, and you will have a chance to taste Dr. Pike's latest plant invention for yourself.

A. Invent your own new food! Choose two common fruits or vegetables to combine to produce a new taste treat or a health benefit. Provide a drawing of your new food, along with a new name and a description of its benefits to humans. How will you market your new food to the public?

B. Many horror movies have been made through the years about monster plants that take over the world. Write a plot in which the plant you invented in the assignment above develops unexpected and amazing powers. What happens to your scientific creation? Write your story on a sheet of notebook paper.

C. Creative speakers of the English language splice words together the same way Dr. Pike combines vegetable genes. Many of these blends, also known as portmanteau words, become standard over time. For each portmanteau below, give the two words that formed it.

1. smog _____
2. motel _____
3. brunch _____
4. scurry _____
5. scrunch _____
6. chortle _____

D. What began as fun in Dr. Pike's childhood became his adult profession. What did you especially like to do when you were a small child? How might that interest develop into a career? Write your thoughts on the back of this sheet.

Name _____

The Cannonball Sisters

To the circus crowd that day in 1942, the girls looked like conventional teenagers. But as a fanfare blared, Egle Victoria and Duina Zacchini climbed into the mouth of a 23-foot-long cannon. With a flash of smoke and a thunderous explosion, they hurtled high into the circus tent at 200 miles an hour, the first females ever to perform this amazing stunt.

The sisters were the youngest members of an eminent circus family. Their father, Edmondo Zacchini, had perfected a cannon that used compressed air to launch a human being. When everything went right, a person could soar 100 feet into the air and land in a net 200 feet away. If things went wrong, injury could easily occur. Crowds thronged to see the amazing stunt. First Edmondo's brother and nephews, then his sons served as "human cannonballs." But the outbreak of World War II spelled the act's finale; all the young Zacchini men left to join the army. That's when Egle Victoria and Duina asked for the cannonball jobs.

With great misgiving, Edmondo agreed. The girls trained for weeks. When it was time for their first practice shot, Edmondo held his breath, steeled for the worst. But Egle Victoria and Duina were sensational! They brought new elegance to the stunt, turning half-somersaults as they flew through the air. The girls became the star attraction and continued performing long after they married and had children of their own. Today, their grandchildren carry on the proud Zacchini tradition, amazing crowds with their feats of daring as "human cannonballs."

A. Match these vocabulary riddles with the correct answers.

_____ 1. A Mexican food ending is . . . .   a. a sweet feat
_____ 2. A crowd of weight-lifters is . . . .   b. a normal formal
_____ 3. A candy-maker's accomplishment is . . . . c. a tamale finale
_____ 4. An hour exam packed into 30 minutes is . . . . d. a compressed test
_____ 5. A conventional ballroom dance is . . . .   e. a strong throng

B. Finish this newspaper ad: "Help Wanted: Young person willing to train to be human cannonball in circus act. Must be . . . ." Include all traits—physical, mental, and emotional—that you believe are necessary for this job. Write your ad on the back of this sheet.

C. In an old movie musical, a girl sings to her boyfriend, "Anything you can do, I can do better." Choose a topic below on the battle of the sexes.
   1. Research one of these convention-breaking females: Sally Ride, Marie Curie, Anne Boney, Nellie Bly, Sojourner Truth, Annie Oakley.
   2. How do people respond to a person who does a job normally held by the opposite sex? What are the advantages/disadvantages?

Name _____

The Power of Observation

"Elementary, my dear Watson!" For Sherlock Holmes' mystery fans, those are well-known words. At the end of every case, the storybook detective patiently explains each clue to his less-observant friend, Dr. Watson. In story after story, readers learn, the secret to Holmes' great detective work is simply a matter of intelligent observation. What most readers do not know, however, is that the character of Sherlock Holmes was based on a real person who had trained himself to notice small details that most people overlook.

Before writing the Sherlock Holmes mysteries, Arthur Conan Doyle had trained as a doctor in Scotland. One of his professors, Dr. Joseph Bell, stressed the role of observation in medicine. A good doctor, the professor claimed, could often diagnose a patient's problem simply by noticing details. To prove his point, Dr. Bell would invite strangers to class. By studying their hands, faces, clothing, accents, and manners, Dr. Bell could spell out the facts of their lives with incredible accuracy. To the students, his powers seemed almost magical. "It was really elementary, gentlemen," he always replied modestly before explaining how he arrived at the facts.

Years later, searching for a worthy protagonist for his mysteries, Arthur Conan Doyle remembered his old professor and patterned the character of Sherlock Holmes after him. The stories became popular immediately upon publication. To this day, readers enjoy testing their own powers of observation against those of the perceptive Sherlock Holmes.

A. Besides detective and doctor, list five other occupations in which keen powers of observation are necessary. Explain.

B. Choose a partner and stage a Sherlock Holmes observation test. Collect a group of small items and display them on a tray. Give your partner 30 seconds to study the items. While the other player looks away, remove and arrange some of the items. Can your partner correctly identify the changes?

C. Choose a person who will give you permission to do a detailed study of his or her outward appearance. Spend time observing your subject closely. Write down details about the person's face, hands, hair, clothing, shoes, physical condition, posture, movements, habits, and accent. Write up your findings, making connections between the details you observed and facts about the person's life. How accurate are your observations? Would you make a good Sherlock Holmes?

D. Read a Sherlock Holmes story for yourself. On a sheet of notebook paper, write a brief summary and evaluate Holmes' skill as a master observer.

Name _____

All for the Love of Sugar

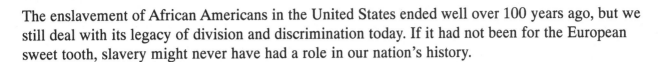

The enslavement of African Americans in the United States ended well over 100 years ago, but we still deal with its legacy of division and discrimination today. If it had not been for the European sweet tooth, slavery might never have had a role in our nation's history.

Almost every ancient culture practiced some form of slavery. Victors in war brought home captives and forced them to work, farming or producing goods in Egypt, Persia, China, India, Africa, Greece, and Rome. The spread of Islam brought crusading European Christians to the Holy Land in A.D. 1000, where they tasted sugar for the first time. Returning home, enterprising Crusaders established Europe's first sugar plantations along the Mediterranean Sea. European workers could not keep up with the demand for the new taste sensation, so owners turned to slave labor to increase their production. The first sugar slaves came from Russia, but they were soon replaced by some Africans purchased from the Arabs. They proved to be superior workers, strong and healthy. By the 1400s Spanish and Portuguese captains sailed directly to Africa to import slaves for the booming sugar trade; no other racial group was considered strong enough to handle the intense labor.

Next, Europe reached across the Atlantic to establish new sugar colonies in America. For a short time, plantation owners attempted to enslave the large indigenous populations. But the New World Indians lacked resistance to European diseases and thousands died. So the colonial sugar planters turned once again to Africa. Over the next 300 years, more than 12 million slaves arrived in the New World. Europe's demand for sugar and its derivatives, molasses and rum, created a triangular trade route that was highly profitable. Ships carried manufactured goods, such as cloth or guns, from Europe to the west coast of Africa, where the goods were traded for slaves. From Africa, the ships crossed the Atlantic and sold their human cargo in the West Indies for as much as $1,000 per slave. Captains returning home loaded up with Caribbean sugar products to sell in European markets.

Of the 12 million slaves brought to the New World prior to 1800, only six percent went to North America; the rest worked in Brazil, Cuba, Haiti, and Jamaica. Sugar planters in Louisiana and Georgia continued to depend on large numbers of slaves, but with the growth of industry in the North, slavery no longer played as essential a role in the nation's economy. Then Eli Whitney invented the cotton gin, a machine that did the work of 50 people, removing the seeds from bolls of cotton. The demand for cotton eclipsed the sugar trade overnight and became the money crop that drove American slavery forward. Planters needed ever-increasing numbers of workers to feed the new machines. By 1860 there were 4 million slaves working the cotton fields of the South. Built by sugar and boosted by cotton, the institution of slavery grew into a wedge that would shortly splinter the nation.

Name _____

All for the Love of Sugar ➤

A. For each word write the letter of the correct definition.

_____ 1. legacy
_____ 2. enterprising
_____ 3. Crusaders
_____ 4. indigenous
_____ 5. derivative
_____ 6. cargo
_____ 7. boll
_____ 8. eclipsed

a. the freight on a ship
b. to hide or overtake
c. an inheritance
d. given to courage and energy
e. the pod of a plant
f. European soldiers who fought to recover Jerusalem from Moslems in the eleventh through thirteenth centuries
g. anything obtained from another substance
h. growing in a country, native

B. Fill in the blanks below with the vocabulary words above.
   1. The cold cream ladies love to smooth on their faces is a petroleum _____.
   2. Edwin Thomas Booth was a talented stage actor, but his fame was _____ by his brother's assassination of Abraham Lincoln.
   3. The meat-eating Venus flytrap is _____ only to a small section of southeastern North Carolina.
   4. I will always treasure the _____ of faith handed down by my family.
   5. Rats hidden in merchant ships' _____ spread deadly diseases from country to country.
   6. The _____ youngsters set up a lemonade stand beside the hot, dusty construction site.
   7. Picking out the seeds enmeshed in a _____ of cotton is tedious work.
   8. _____ returning from the Middle East brought home a gambling game called *pachisi*, from which the modern board game Parcheesi was developed.

C. What if? On the back of this sheet, finish each sentence with a conclusion you can draw from the facts.
   1. If the Moslems had never captured Jerusalem . . . .
   2. If the Russians first used on sugar cane farms had proven to be good workers . . . .
   3. If Eli Whitney had invented the conveyor belt instead of the cotton gin . . . .
   4. If the practice of slavery had never taken root in the United States . . . .
   5. If more of our citizens focused on an individual's inner worth rather than outward appearance . . . .

D. Think and write.
   1. List at least five modern-day conditions that are the legacy of slavery in America. Propose actions you can take in your own community to remedy these conditions.
   2. Suppose you worked as a slave. List and explain at least five strengths you would develop in spite of—or because of—your lack of freedom.

Name _____

Death in the Clouds

It was supposed to be the perfect solution for transporting large numbers of people by air—inexpensive to build and operate, free from the difficulties that plagued the primitive airplanes of the day. Dirigibles, or lighter-than-air ships, were huge shells of fabric filled with gas. Equipped with engines and steering mechanisms, smaller ships ranged in size from 200 to 400 feet long. England and Germany used them for military purposes during World War I, to scout enemy positions and carry bombs. U.S. Navy airships launched and received small fighter airplanes, much like the oceangoing aircraft carriers of later years. Of the nations operating airships during the 1920s and 1930s, Germany had the most success. Its dirigible *Graf Zeppelin* flew more than a million miles and transported 13,000 people over land and sea between 1928 and 1937. With this achievement under its belt, Germany built the largest airship ever, the *Hindenburg*, over 800 feet long and almost 200 feet wide, with room for 100 passengers. But on May 6, 1937, the *Hindenburg* exploded without warning in a huge fireball over Lakehurst, New Jersey.

It had been a routine flight. The ground crew waited patiently at the base of the tall tower where the *Hindenburg* would dock. But as the huge ship neared, it suddenly exploded; despite all safety precautions, the hydrogen gas inside the dirigible ignited. Thirty-five passengers and one ground crewman died in the accident. That crash, coupled with improvements in airplane safety, brought the use of lighter-than-air ships for passenger travel to an end.

A. A subject sentence expresses all the pertinent facts of a reading selection in 15 words or less. It omits minor details and unnecessary articles such as *a* and *the*. Try writing a subject sentence for this selection. Compare your sentence with those written by classmates to choose the most effective one.

B. All the lines in a preposition poem are prepositional phrases. Write one of these poems about the *Hindenburg* explosion. Here is a sample about a happier flight: Into the *Graf Zeppelin*, into my seat, over my village, over the treetops, over the mountains, up in the clouds, into the cool air over the sea, on a gentle ride to my new home on the other side of the world.

C. In 1937 the *Hindenburg* explosion stopped virtually all future dirigible travel. Yet today, when a train wrecks or a plane crashes, life marches on. Why? What has changed since 1937?

Name _____

Quake!

On April 18, 1906, the people of San Francisco surely thought that the world was coming to an end. Ships off the coast of California were the first to feel the violent shock. At 5:10 a.m., a gap in the earth's crust opened along the San Andreas Fault, a crack that stretches 600 miles from Southern California to the Pacific Ocean north of San Francisco. Shock waves moving more than two miles a second quickly hit the shore, tumbling buildings into the ocean, ripping up trees, and heaving pavement into piles of rubble.

Ten seconds later, a second shock struck. The force that rocked the city was greater than all the bombs that would be used in World War II, but the results were similar. The city of mansions and cable cars became a battlefield. Tall buildings collapsed, trains derailed, water and gas lines ruptured. The rich and famous suffered alongside San Francisco's more ordinary citizens. Adventure-writer Jack London battled blaze and rubble along with the international opera star Enrico Caruso and movie actor John Barrymore.

Fanned by ocean winds, fires raged out of control for three days. In desperation, firemen set off massive explosions, leveling entire blocks of the city. Only then did the fires cease. When the smoke cleared, five square miles lay in charred ruins. Seven hundred people died and more than 300,000 were left without homes.

A. Write T for true or F for false.

  _____ 1. San Francisco looked like one bomb had exploded there.
  _____ 2. People had time to seek shelter before the quake hit.
  _____ 3. The quake seemed to affect mainly the wealthy people of the city.
  _____ 4. It took still more destruction to stop the fires set off by the earthquake.
  _____ 5. Four shocks struck the city.

B. Disaster movies are always big at the box office. Use information from the selection to write Scene I for a movie about the San Francisco earthquake, *Frisco Frenzy*.

C. Read to learn more about one of the famous people present for the San Francisco earthquake. Write comments your character might have made during the disaster. Use the back of this sheet.

Name _____

Viral Killer ———————————————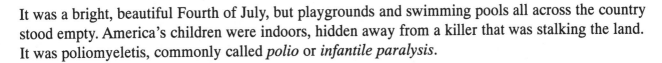

It was a bright, beautiful Fourth of July, but playgrounds and swimming pools all across the country stood empty. America's children were indoors, hidden away from a killer that was stalking the land. It was poliomyeletis, commonly called *polio* or *infantile paralysis*.

No one knew exactly how the disease spread, but it struck with little warning, just a slight fever or headache and sore throat. Polio's effects were devastating, especially to young developing bodies— permanent damage to brain cells and the spinal cord, resulting in muscle weakness and paralysis. In 1915 an outbreak of polio struck 27,000 young Americans, killing 6,000 of them, leaving the rest in leg braces or hooked to breathing machines for life. And polio was not selective. It struck rich and poor, weak and strong, in the city or out on the farm. Franklin D. Roosevelt, who would later serve as president of the United States, was a healthy, 39-year-old father of six when the virus attacked. It paralyzed his back, arms, legs, and hands. Only through great determination and physical exercise did Roosevelt regain the strength to use his upper body and later enter politics. He would never again, however, walk without the help of heavy leg braces and canes.

There was no treatment capable of stopping that early epidemic. After four years of fury, it mysteriously wore itself out. The public relaxed. Then, almost 40 years later, polio struck again, this time much harder. More than 55,000 Americans developed the disease in a single year. Health officials took desperate measures to stop the virus, closing parks, pools, and theaters in 1952. By now, they knew the disease was air-borne. Germs from infected people traveled through the air to enter the noses and mouths of others. "Stay home," doctors said. "That's all we can tell you to do."

Meanwhile, a team of scientists worked frantically to learn more about this killer. Led by Dr. Jonas Salk, they developed a vaccine they believed would immunize healthy people against the polio virus. The vaccine, however, could also cause harmful side effects. With polio striking new victims daily, there was no time to fine-tune the chemistry. Instead, Dr. Salk administered the vaccine to 45 patients already suffering from the disease. Their blood showed increased levels of polio-fighting antibodies, and, miraculously, not one patient developed dangerous side effects.

Under normal circumstances, scientists run thousands of tests before they release a new drug. But after just 45 cases, Dr. Salk immunized himself and his own family to prove his confidence in the vaccine. The possibility for side effects was still there, he knew, but the thousands of lives that could be saved were worth the risk. In 1954 almost two million American children received the shots at school. Within weeks, the vaccine turned the tide. New cases of polio dropped significantly and finally tapered to nothing. The epidemic was over; the killer, polio, had been stopped dead in its tracks.

Viral Killer

A. For each quotation below, write a correct speaker.
   1. "No, I love you too much to let you go to the park just to have fun." _____
   2. "But dear, what if one of our own boys becomes infected? Could you live with yourself, knowing you had purposely exposed him just as part of an experiment?" _____
   3. "Daddy, why does the president walk so funny?" _____
   4. "Nobody has come down with polio in years. It won't matter if my children don't get their shots. There's no virus left, anyway." _____
   5. "Oh no, it's back! I hoped I would never see another patient suffer like those pitiful folks did back in '15." _____

B. There are many people who still remember the polio epidemic of the 1950s. Find someone to interview about those days. Record his or her memories.

C. Dr. Jonas Salk, the hero in this crisis, was a remarkable man. Read about his life and answer these questions on the back of this sheet.
   1. How did Salk get to go to medical school?
   2. How did Salk feel about the cash prizes he was offered for developing the polio vaccine?
   3. What other health problem did Salk research?

D. Beside each statement write the correct era: 1915 or 1950.
   _____ 1. Public places closed down.
   _____ 2. 6,000 people died of polio.
   _____ 3. 55,000 victims contracted polio in one year.
   _____ 4. Doctors learned how the disease spread.
   _____ 5. An experimental vaccine was tested on 45 patients.
   _____ 6. Franklin D. Roosevelt contracted polio.
   _____ 7. Two million schoolchildren were vaccinated.
   _____ 8. Jonas Salk vaccinated his own family.
   _____ 9. Doctors did not understand how the disease spread.
   _____ 10. Patients' blood showed increased levels of antibodies.

E. Problems that cause suffering often make us angry, but putting that anger into words can defuse it. Write a definition poem about a problem that really upsets you: AIDS, cancer, divorce, death, poverty. Your poem should begin with a question and end in a statement, with six to eight lines of powerful description in the middle. Here is a definition poem about polio:
   What is polio?
   It's the iron that imprisons my legs,
   It's the machine that makes my lungs work.
   A thief who steals my muscles
   And leaves jelly in their place.
   Polio hides in every playground,
   A spider waiting for his fly.
   A killer no one can stop,
   Because we don't know what we're looking for.
   That's polio, the disease that I hate.

Name _____

The Johnstown Flood ⬇️

Life was good in Johnstown, Pennsylvania, in 1889. Jobs in the new steel industry provided a comfortable life for the city's 25,000 residents. Lake Conemaugh nearby guaranteed plenty of fresh water as well as lovely scenery. But after two weeks of rain, Johnstown was a soggy mess. Then heavy rain began again on May 31. At 1 p.m., an alarm sounded at the dam at Lake Conemaugh, warning that water levels were approaching dangerous highs. The 90-foot-thick dam had just recently been rebuilt, so the people of Johnstown were confident it would hold, in spite of the weather. Shortly after 3 p.m., however, the dam burst, sending a 20-foot-high wall of water down on the city. Residents heard an approaching roar, but there was little time to make preparations. Floodwaters engulfed the city, picking up buildings, trains, and factories that stood in their path. Many people were instantly swept away. Others managed to get their families atop chunks of floating debris until the waters abated. The mountain of wreckage rushing downstream soon grew over 30 feet tall. Two thousand, two hundred people died and property worth more than $10 million was lost. It was the first time in American history a city had faced a flood of this magnitude. With all the ingenuity American engineers could muster, the residents of Johnstown rebuilt the dam, but it burst again in 1936 and overflowed in 1977, taking lives and damaging millions of dollars' worth of property both times.

A. For each vocabulary word listed below, circle the best synonym.
1. engulf: sink, overwhelm, wash, ripple
2. debris: property, baggage, excess, trash
3. abate: lessen, increase, flow, dilute
4. magnitude: cost, greatness, type, nature
5. muster: assemble, buy, imagine, announce

B. Match each vocabulary riddle to the correct answer.
_____ 1. A giant gentleman is . . .   a. to be flooded with blood
_____ 2. A trash fight in the cafeteria is . . .   b. hate abate
_____ 3. To be engulfed in gore is . . .   c. to muster the dusters
_____ 4. To collect dirt removers is . . .   d. a dude of great magnitude
_____ 5. Kindness and courtesy make . . .   e. a debris jubilee

C. Choose one of the news headlines below and write a report on the situation in Johnstown. Give accurate dates from the selection and add your own creative details to make the story interesting.
1. Johnstown Wonders, Where's the Ark?
2. Mother Nature 3, Johnstown 0
3. Travels by Rooftop
4. Twice as Nice: Johnstown Rebuilds Dam

Name _____

Ordeal by Hunger ➤

California! To George and Jacob Donner, it was the land of dreams, the place where they could make a fresh start and prosper. So, in the summer of 1846, the brothers packed up their families and said goodbye to their neighbors in Illinois. They joined a large wagon train, hoping to reach California before winter. The trip across the plains went smoothly, and, by the time they reached Utah, the Donner brothers felt confident enough to strike out on their own. Twenty-three wagons, 82 men, women, and children in all, took a shortcut to the south of the Great Salt Lake. Cutting a new trail took longer than they anticipated, and Indian attacks slowed them down. By the time the group reached the Sierra Nevada Mountains on October 31, their supplies were dangerously low. To make things worse, an early winter had blocked the only pass through the treacherous peaks. The Donners built log shelters and waited for a break in the weather. But snow continued to fall and many of their oxen, the group's main source of food, wandered off. By December the settlers were eating twigs and mice. Fifteen adults left to get help, while those at the camp boiled and ate shoes. A small rescue party finally arrived and carried out 23 settlers, most of them children. The remainder began dying of starvation. In desperation, the living ate the flesh from the dead bodies of their friends. By April 22 the last living settlers were rescued. Of the Donner party, only 47 survived the horrible ordeal.

A. Write T for true or F for false.

_____ 1. It is a fact that George and Jacob Donner were poor leaders.

_____ 2. Unexpected problems slowed the Donners down.

_____ 3. The stranded settlers made no effort to find other sources of food before resorting to cannibalism.

_____ 4. Less than half of the original Donner party survived.

_____ 5. There was only one way wagons could get over the Sierra Nevadas.

_____ 6. The Donners had planned to live off what they could find along the trail.

_____ 7. Winters are often long and hard in the Sierra Nevadas.

_____ 8. Some in the Donner party preferred death to cannibalism.

B. Refusing to eat the flesh of his own kind is one of the few traits that separates man from beast. On the back of this sheet, list at least five differences and five similarities between humans and animals.

C. Imagine that you are a member of the Donner party. Write journal entries for the final few days that express your thoughts and feelings. Do you eat your friends' bodies, or do you choose to die instead?

Name _____

Island Mystery

In the scope of world history, the return of 15 captives to their homeland seems like a detail too small to record. But for tiny Easter Island in the South Pacific, the event brought about a disaster of major proportions. The island, only 47 square miles large, is famous for the enormous stone statues, known as moai, which were erected by early inhabitants. Six hundred large, angular heads guard the island, each of them measuring about 20 feet high and weighing over 80 metric tons. The statues were designed to sit on raised stone platforms covered with mysterious picture-writing. No one knows how the heads were made or why.

In 1862 Peru, some 2,000 miles to the east of Easter Island, needed slaves to work in its cotton and sugar cane plantations. Traders captured most of the islanders, about 1,400 in all, and sold them to wealthy planters. Working in altitudes and climates to which they were unaccustomed, the Easter Island slaves began dying at alarming rates. A year later, only 100 were still alive, and some kind soul decided to return them to their native shores. On the voyage back, 85 died of smallpox. The remaining 15 disembarked and promptly spread the deadly disease through the small number of their kinsmen still living on Easter Island. A handful survived, but none of them remembered to pass the meaning of the stone statues on to their children. Today islanders and scientists alike struggle to interpret the strange symbol-writing left behind in the hope that someday it will give up the secret of the moai.

A. Loss of knowledge, whenever and wherever it occurs, is a terrible tragedy. Put yourself in the Easter Islanders' shoes; imagine a crisis that wipes out all knowledge of books and reading. What would it be like to be surrounded by books and not understand what they were for? Write a story describing your feelings.

B. What happened first? Number the events in order from 1 to 7.
_____ 1. Returning islanders spread smallpox.
_____ 2. Slaves captured and taken to Peru.
_____ 3. Knowledge of moai dies.
_____ 4. Surviving slaves sent home.
_____ 5. Moai erected on platforms covered with symbol-writing.
_____ 6. Population nearly wiped out.
_____ 7. Islanders made poor slaves.

C. Check a reference to see how the Easter Island heads look. Then choose one of the fictitious headlines below to illustrate on drawing paper.
1. Astronaut Announces: "Matching Moai on Moon!"
2. Easter Island Giant's Checkerboard
3. Camper Cracks Code of Quiet Heads
4. Island Heads Squash Hopes for Healthy Tourist Season

Unlucky Ladies

Tornado, flood, cancer, earthquake, riot, shortages, and high prices—when disaster strikes, we look for something or someone to blame. Whose fault is it? To get the answer, we must go all the way back to the very beginning of time. In the beginning, so the ancient stories say, it was a woman's curiosity that made pain and suffering one of the facts of life for all of us.

The Bible tells of Eve, who wondered about the fruit hanging from an off-limits tree. Created in love, blessed with a mate, and given a perfect garden in which to live, Eve should have had no complaints. But curiosity got the best of her, and she plucked the forbidden fruit. The consequences were immediate: expulsion from the garden, a lifetime sentence to hard labor, and the sorrow of knowing she had brought this same fate on all her children.

In a Greek myth with striking similarities, the woman is named *Pandora,* meaning "all gifts." Angry that the first men had stolen fire from Mt. Olympus, Zeus commanded the creation of a woman gifted with beauty, charm, intelligence, and wit. Men's punishment would be to fall in love with her. In spite of repeated warnings from the gods, Pandora was curious about a jar. When she opened it, every evil known to man escaped, to fill the earth forever after. (In later versions of the story, the jar became a box.)

A. A limerick tells a humorous story in a verse of five lines. Lines one and two rhyme with line five; lines three and four also rhyme. On the back of this sheet, retell the stories of Eve and Pandora in limerick form. Use as many verses as needed; add your own creative or funny details. Here are some starters:
   There was a young lady named Eve . . .
   The Evils were kept in a jar . . .
   The apple that hung from the tree . . .
   "Don't touch!" commanded King Zeus . . .

B. The story of Pandora continues on a happier note. When all the evils had escaped from the jar, Pandora found one creature left inside she could hold onto: hope. On another sheet of paper, write your own ending to the story, describing hope and explaining how it helps Pandora.

C. Nearly every culture has its own stories explaining the origins of evil, death, war, unkindness, quarreling. Choose one of the cultures listed below and research its stories. Be prepared to tell a story to the class.
   Native American
   African
   Middle European
   Asian
   U.S. Appalachian

Name _____

Blood Ties

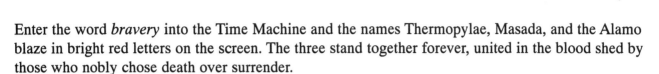

Enter the word *bravery* into the Time Machine and the names Thermopylae, Masada, and the Alamo blaze in bright red letters on the screen. The three stand together forever, united in the blood shed by those who nobly chose death over surrender.

Thermopylae was a narrow mountain pass on the road into ancient Greece. To its south the great city-states of Athens and Sparta hung like ripe plums. King Xerxes of Persia, ever looking to expand his empire, attacked in 480 B.C. The decisive battle took place where a tiny band of Greeks stood guarding the narrow passageway. The well-armed Persians outnumbered the defenders more than twelve to one, odds that seemed hopeless. But the plucky Greeks held the enemy off for two entire days, until a traitor showed the Persians a secret trail. The Greeks suddenly found themselves surrounded but still refused to yield. They fought to the bloody end, buying time for the soldiers preparing the defense of Athens down the road. To this day, Greeks consider it their finest hour.

Like Thermopylae, Masada, a fortress perched on the rocks of southern Israel, was the scene of great suffering and incredible courage. For six years Jewish patriots had fought to break Roman dictatorship of their land. Like angry hornets, tiny bands of rebels would swarm from hiding places to sting the enemy, then vanish from view. The Romans were determined to end this embarrassment. They tracked down a large band of rebels holed up in the old Masada fortress, 960 men, women, and children in all. The Romans first attempted to starve the Jews out, but for three years the rebels managed to sneak in food. When that failed, the soldiers constructed a huge ramp up the mountain and launched a massive assault. Capture or death for the rebels was inevitable. Rather than give in to their hated enemy, the Jews of Masada killed first their children, then themselves.

The siege of the Alamo was smaller than those of Masada and Thermopylae, but it had great significance in the war for Texan independence. By 1836 American settlers in Texas wanted to cut ties with the Mexican government. To put down the rebellion, Mexican General Santa Anna, in a surprise move, assembled 5,000 troops just outside San Antonio. About 180 Texans managed to make it to an old mission, the Alamo, where they could take shots at Santa Anna's men. The Texans' leader sent urgent requests for aid, while others, including famous trailblazers Jim Bowie and Davy Crockett, fired sparingly to conserve their small stockpile of ammunition. Help never came. The bullets ran out twelve days later, and on March 6 Mexican troops scaled the walls. Furious at the Americans' resistance in the face of overwhelming odds, Santa Anna commanded that no prisoners be taken. It was death or surrender for the men in the Alamo. The Americans fought valiantly to the end, swinging their empty rifles like clubs. None of the men survived, but the defeat spurred other Texans on to fight even harder. A few months later, Mexico was forced to grant the settlers their independence.

Blood Ties

Name _____

A. Code each statement below T for Thermopylae, M for Masada, and A for Alamo. Some statements may apply to more than one place.

_____ 1. Children died here.
_____ 2. Soldiers' fight-til-death encouraged their comrades in battles that followed.
_____ 3. Took place in tight quarters.
_____ 4. Attack from behind defeated these guardians.
_____ 5. Dared to defy those who ruled them.
_____ 6. Men whose accomplishments had made them famous did not shrink from this battle.
_____ 7. Honored to this day for the bravery displayed and sacrifice made.
_____ 8. Fought on rocky ground.
_____ 9. Women bravely took a stand beside their husbands.
_____ 10. Ammunition ran out.
_____ 11. Lasted three years.
_____ 12. Lasted three days.
_____ 13. Lasted 13 days.

B. A *eulogy* is a dramatic speech given in honor of someone who has died. It reminds listeners of the person's character and the contributions he or she made while living. Choose a warrior from Thermopylae, Masada, or the Alamo to eulogize. Create a name for your character and describe what he or she did, but omit the name of the battle. After you have written your speech, share it with your classmates. See if they can match your warrior with the correct conflict.

C. Think and answer on the back of this sheet.
1. Is death always the bravest choice? When does it take more courage to live than it does to die?
2. Why do people cheer for the underdog? How does an underdog inspire us?
3. The warriors of Thermopylae, Masada, and the Alamo paid the highest price of all—their lives—for freedom. List at least five things that people today might be willing to die for. Check the ones that you personally consider worthy causes.

D. Choose a topic to research and write about:
1. Jim Bowie
2. Davy Crockett
3. Sparta's soldiers
4. Xerxes I
5. Eleazer Ben Jair and the Sicarii (Masada)

E. Look in the newspaper for three articles about current situations that could be compared to Thermopylae, Masada, or the Alamo. For each event, explain the similarities and differences. From reading the articles, what can you conclude about modern man, bravery, and love of freedom?

Name _____

Telescope Through Time

"Do not worry! After you have lived here a while, you become accustomed to the shaking." With these words the residents of ancient Pompeii reassured all those who came to their small, pleasant city. Wealthy patricians, eager to escape the crowds of Naples and Rome, built villas here, drawn by the mild, sunny weather. With a healthy trade in wine, oil, and bread from nearby farms, the city offered all the conveniences of ancient living: an amphitheater, a gladiator's court, temples to the gods, and public baths. Even the scenery was great, offering a view of the harbor in one direction, Mount Vesuvius less than a mile away in another. The ancient volcano had lain dormant during the entire time Pompeii was settled and growing to city-size.

Beginning in A.D. 63, Vesuvius showed signs of coming to life again. On and off for 16 years, the mountain rumbled and the ground beneath residents' feet shook. Occasionally, statues fell and a roof collapsed, but life in Pompeii rolled on. Then on August 24, A.D. 79, citizens awoke to a rapidly darkening sky. An acrid smell filled the air; the ground shook repeatedly. Alarmed, some folks packed up valuables and headed for boats anchored in the harbor. Others continued about their daily routine, certain that this episode would soon pass. Neither group had much time to worry—Vesuvius violently erupted in mid-morning. The Pompeiians tried to flee, choking on smoke, dodging the stones that rained from the sky. Some escaped; many others died in the noxious fumes, buried under thick layers of hot ash.

When Vesuvius finally settled down, all that remained visible of Pompeii were the tops of tall stone columns. The ash cooled and hardened, creating a tomb where life had once bustled. More eruptions occurred. Eventually erosion covered the site with soil. And so the city slept through the centuries, buried and forgotten. But in 1748, a farmer digging in his vineyard struck an underground wall. Intrigued, experts began to excavate, and what they found over the years astonished them. Amid the ruins beneath their feet were people-shaped holes. By pouring plaster into these holes, they were able to make casts of over 2,000 Pompeiians who had perished when Vesuvius erupted.

These silent statues bring the tragedy to life once more, reminding us that disaster struck with little warning. There is a baker overcome as he kneads the day's bread, an expression of agony plain to read on his face. Here are the bodies of a boy and his dog, together forever. A loyal servant laden with parcels heads for the harbor—never to make it. The details preserved in plaster reveal how people dressed and wore their hair, how they decorated their homes, what they served on their tables. Every year, as more of the site is excavated, new information about daily life in old Pompeii comes to light. What was a terrible tragedy has become a telescope by which we can view our not-so-ancient past.

Name _____

Telescope Through Time ➤

A. For each word write the letter of the correct definition.

_____ 1. patrician   a. sharp, harsh, bitter
_____ 2. amphitheater   b. to dig out
_____ 3. gladiator   c. one who fights for public amusement
_____ 4. dormant   d. an occurrence
_____ 5. acrid   e. an aristocrat
_____ 6. episode   f. a circular building with tiers of seats
_____ 7. noxious   g. hurtful, unhealthy
_____ 8. excavate   h. inactive

B. Match these vocabulary riddles with the correct answers.

_____ 1. a reptile wrestler   a. a fishin' patrician
_____ 2. acrid margarine   b. a deadly medley
_____ 3. equipment for excavating large holes   c. a dormant ornament
_____ 4. an aristocratic angler   d. a toad episode
_____ 5. a occurrence involving tailless amphibians   e. a gator gladiator
_____ 6. a noxious collection of songs   f. bitter butter
_____ 7. a Christmas decoration in March   g. digging rigging

C. Circle the best title for the selection.
   1. Volcanoes of the World
   2. Life in Old Pompeii
   3. Buried City
   4. Roman Tragedy
   5. A Short History of Vesuvius

D. Look up each famous volcano below and write where and when it erupted.
   1. El Chichon _____   6. Cotopaxi _____
   2. Hibokhibok _____   7. Mt. St. Helens _____
   3. Paricutin _____   8. Mt. Etna _____
   4. Krakatoa _____   9. Mont Pelee _____
   5. Mount Katmai _____

E. The twin Latin roots, *pater* and *mater*, mean "father" and "mother." They give us modern words that also look like twins. For each word pair listed below, explain the definitions. (Not every pair will have identical meanings.)
   1. patriarch/matriarch   4. patron/matron
   2. patrimony/matrimony   5. paternity/maternity
   3. patronym/matronym   6. patricide/matricide
                                 7. patriarchy/matriarchy

Drastic Drama

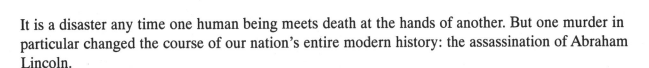

It is a disaster any time one human being meets death at the hands of another. But one murder in particular changed the course of our nation's entire modern history: the assassination of Abraham Lincoln.

The ink had barely dried on the document ending the Civil War the night that Lincoln and his wife attended a play in Washington, D.C. At last, the end to four, long years of bitterness and hardship was in sight. Lincoln had just been elected to another term as president and yearned to knit the North and South back together into one nation. The people, regardless of skin color, place of birth, or politics, had suffered enough, Lincoln said. It was time to look ahead, to build a new and better society. As Mr. Lincoln watched *Our American Cousin*, a vision of equality and justice for all swirled in his head.

But others could not put the heartaches of the past four years behind them so easily. Many across the burned fields of the South held Lincoln personally responsible for their horrendous loss. A talented young actor, John Wilkes Booth, was part of a secret organization that planned revenge. The group plotted to kidnap or kill Lincoln and his advisors. Ironically, Lincoln, a fan of the theater, greatly admired Booth and tried to attend any plays in which the actor appeared.

The night of April 14, 1865, fate presented Booth with the opportunity to carry out his plan. The president's bodyguard left his post in the theater to get a drink. Booth silently stepped up behind Lincoln's seat and shot him once in the back of the head with a derringer. Jumping down to the stage, Booth caught his spur in a Union flag and broke his leg. Crazed with adrenaline, he continued to flee, shouting a message to the stunned audience: Sic Semper Tyrannis, Thus Always to Tyrants, the Virginia state motto. Booth made his escape on a horse he had tied outside Ford's Theatre, but with his broken leg, he did not get far. Soldiers found him twelve days later, cowering in a barn nearby.

Meanwhile, doctors carried Lincoln to a home across the street from the theater. There, they worked all night to save his life, but the president died early the next morning. Andrew Johnson took the oath of office a few hours later and inherited the enormous problems of rebuilding the nation. The new president worked hard to implement Lincoln's optimistic plans, helping the Southern states get back on their feet and protecting former slaves. But he lacked Lincoln's forcefulness and leadership; almost immediately, Congress voted down the mild policies. Instead, laws were passed that one by one usurped the rights ex-slaves had gained. Long into the 1900s, many African Americans living in the South were little better off than they had been under the slave system. Lincoln's dream for justice and equality died with him, not to live again until the civil rights movement of the 1960s.

Drastic Drama

Name _____

A. For each word write the letter of the correct definition.

_____ 1. yearn   a. hopeful
_____ 2. derringer   b. shrinking with fear
_____ 3. crazed   c. to be filled with longing
_____ 4. adrenaline   d. to put into practice
_____ 5. cowering   e. to take away another's powers or position
_____ 6. implement   f. a short-barreled pistol
_____ 7. optimistic   g. a compound that stimulates the heart
_____ 8. usurp   h. to be temporarily insane

B. Fill in each blank below with one of the vocabulary words.
1. The gangster had a _____ concealed in his pocket.
2. A young prince is careful never to _____ the powers of his father, the king.
3. How will you _____ your self-improvement plan?
4. Every strange sound sent him _____ under the bedcovers.
5. We _____ for modern leaders who will be more like the heroes from the pages of our nation's history.
6. The rosy sunset made us _____ about the picnic scheduled for the next day.
7. People _____ on drugs or alcohol cannot make responsible decisions.
8. _____ is what helps our bodies act quickly in emergency situations.

C. Circle the best title for the reading selection.
1. The Booths: First Family of Theater
2. Andrew Johnson's Brick Wall
3. The Death of Hope
4. Our American Cousin
5. Death to Tyrants

D. Code each statement below L for Lincoln, J for Johnson, or B for Booth. Some statements may apply to more than one person.
_____ 1. thought Lincoln was a tyrant.
_____ 2. loved the theater.
_____ 3. motivated people to work together.
_____ 4. hoped to heal the nation.
_____ 5. ended a dream with his deed.
_____ 6. tried but failed.
_____ 7. lost his life in the days following the Civil War.
_____ 8. was president.

Name _____

The Day the Dollar Died ————————————

The word *disaster* calls to mind storm, accident, warfare, or disease. One of the largest disasters in world history involved all of these—the Great Depression. In ten years' time, this financial crisis touched every home in America. It brought international trade to a screeching halt and toppled governments around the world. Events snowballed to include mass suicide, malnutrition, homelessness, ethnic persecution, drought, and dust storm. The disaster even set in motion conflicts that escalated into World War II.

The crisis officially began on October 24, 1929, "Black Thursday." Over $9 billion was lost in the stock market on that day alone. Overnight, there was no money to finance new business or industry; to pay salaries, mortgages, and debts; to keep banks, factories, and stores open. By 1933 over 13 million Americans were out of work. Unable to pay rent or buy food, thousands of families hit the road, looking for any way to earn money. To eat, they begged, took handouts from mission organizations, and did without. They lived in their cars or built shacks from boxes and flattened tin cans. Former business executives sold apples on the street or shined shoes. Many simply could not cope with the conditions and, in despair, committed suicide. With no money for medical care, others died of diseases that simple treatments could have cured. For a time, farmers were somewhat better off. No markets existed for their crops, but they could at least grow food to feed their families. Then droughts and dust storms hit the Midwest, drying up even their vegetable gardens and cow pastures.

Overseas, Germans suffering from the depression looked for someone to blame. Adolf Hitler claimed that Jewish businessmen were overcharging their neighbors and began his awful practices of discrimination and elimination. In Japan, leaders seeking to improve their hard-hit economy invaded China. Using military force, they built mines and industries and forced the Chinese to generate income for Japan. These atrocities would eventually result in World War II.

The Great Depression raged until the federal government took drastic measures. Under President Franklin D. Roosevelt's strong leadership, Congress passed laws that provided welfare for the neediest of Americans. Reforms to protect the public from shaky banks and businesses were set up, and many government jobs were created, building bridges, dams, and schools across the country. As people began to earn small wages again, their confidence in America increased. Soon, they were putting money back into the banks and saving to invest in their own businesses again. Factories and stores reopened. But recuperation was slow. Fifteen percent of America's workers still did not have jobs in 1940. It took the outbreak of World War II to bring an end to the depression. Factories went into overtime to produce the equipment and supplies the United States needed to go to war. At last, there were jobs for all; the worst financial crisis in modern history was over.

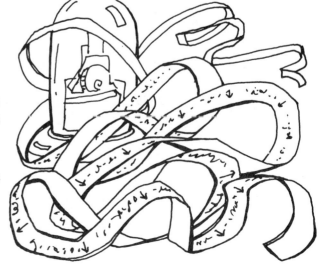

Name _____

The Day the Dollar Died ➤

A. Fact or opinion? Write F for fact or O for opinion on the blank.

_____ 1. The Great Depression was harder on people than World War II.

_____ 2. City folks worried more than farmers did.

_____ 3. The financial crisis caused many successful businessmen to commit suicide.

_____ 4. People were embarrassed to ask for handouts of food.

_____ 5. Lack of cash caused Japan to attack China.

_____ 6. It was better to stay home during the depression rather than traveling the country looking for work.

_____ 7. If World War II had not started, the depression would have continued for many years.

_____ 8. Only Franklin D. Roosevelt knew how to end the financial crisis.

_____ 9. The U.S. government created many jobs during the depression.

_____ 10. These government jobs did very little to improve life for those suffering in the crisis.

B. Hard times can teach important lessons. If another Great Depression were to occur, discuss positive things you think your family could learn.

C. There are many wise proverbs regarding money. On white paper, draw an illustration that explains one of these sayings.

1. A penny saved is a penny earned.
2. A fool and his money are soon parted.
3. Penny wise and pound foolish.
4. Saving for a rainy day.
5. Neither a borrower nor a lender be.
6. Early to bed, early to rise, makes a man healthy, wealthy, and wise.

D. For each word write the letter of the correct definition.

_____ 1. topple	a.	payment on a large debt
_____ 2. ethnic	b.	a long dry spell
_____ 3. drought	c.	a return to health and stability
_____ 4. escalate	d.	to cause to fall
_____ 5. mortgage	e.	a brutal deed
_____ 6. discrimination	f.	relating to different races of people
_____ 7. atrocity	g.	act of treating one group differently from another
_____ 8. invest	h.	to put funds into a business to profit
_____ 9. recuperation	i.	to increase in intensity

Name _____

The Trail of Tears

Where others had chosen resistance and extinction, they chose compromise. Five Native-American tribes of the Southeast—Cherokee, Creek, Chickasaw, Choctaw, and Seminole—put aside tradition to live in the same manner as their white neighbors. The prosperous farms and peaceful settlements throughout the Carolinas, Georgia, and Florida testified to their hard work and cooperative spirit. But these virtues were not protection enough from white greed. In 1830 the United States ordered the tribes to surrender their farms and move to Indian Territory, in what is now Oklahoma. Tribal leaders presented lengthy objections before the Supreme Court and won their case, but the removal policy remained in force. In May 1838 troops began forcibly removing families from their homes. Whites lined up along the road to shout insults at those departing; they could not wait to get their hands on the vacated land. Army officers assured the Indians that, as payment for their farms, they would receive adequate supplies for the trip West. The 600-mile trek had barely begun when it became obvious that officials could not or would not meet the most basic needs of food and clothing. The onset of winter meant endless days of forced marching in miserable weather. Armed guards made certain that no one lagged behind or left the trail. Of the 15,000 people who began the journey, more than 4,000 died along the way. Their families buried them in unmarked graves beside the road they began to call "The Trail Where They Cried."

A. Circle the statement that best expresses the truth of this paragraph. Give reasons for your choice.
   1. Compromise is often just another name for surrender.
   2. Compromise is only as good as the honor of those making it.
   3. In the name of civilization and progress, the U.S. government stole from those it considered less than civilized.
   4. He who fights and walks away lives to fight another day.

B. It is depressing to read about man's cruelty to man. Why should we remember the mistakes of history? On the back of this sheet, give at least three reasons.

C. Many white settlers traveled this same trail to stake out new homes in the wilderness. Compare and contrast the two journeys.

D. Research to learn more about one of the following:
   1. Chief John Ross
   2. General Stand Watie
   3. Dancer Maria Tallchief
   4. Sequoyah
   5. Humorist Will Rogers

Name _____

Blazing City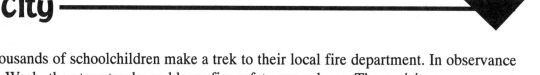

Every October, thousands of schoolchildren make a trek to their local fire department. In observance of Fire Prevention Week, they tour trucks and learn fire safety procedures. These visits commemorate one of the worst disasters in American history—the Great Chicago Fire of 1871. According to legend, the conflagration began when a cow kicked over a lantern in a barn. No one knows for certain, but the factors that fanned the blaze into a raging inferno are certain. The first problem was the city itself. Chicago was the lumber capital of the world. Houses, stores, factories, churches, even streets and sidewalks were made of wood. Another factor was the wind. Built on Lake Michigan, Chicago is known as "The Windy City" for the strong breezes that blow across the water. The final straw was dry weather; it had not rained in weeks. When the first sparks fell on Sunday, October 8, the wooden city ignited like kindling. Three hours later, twenty blocks of houses were burning. Horse-drawn fire engines raced to the scene, but there was too much wind, too much wood, too little equipment, even too little water pressure to do much good. Panic-stricken families sought refuge in the chilly waters of Lake Michigan. The fire burned all the next day, slowing only when rain began to fall on Monday evening. A four-mile section of the city was gone, 300 lives were lost, and 18,000 buildings destroyed. Chicago's great loss led to stringent standards for fireproof buildings, alarms, equipment, and water systems.

A. Write T for true or F for false.
  _____ 1. It is certain that a cow started the Chicago fire.
  _____ 2. Most of Chicago's buildings were made of brick.
  _____ 3. Other cities learned a lesson from Chicago's fire.
  _____ 4. Chicago was well-prepared for a large fire.
  _____ 5. There is never much air movement over Chicago.

B. The sentences below contain vocabulary words from the selection. Code each one C for correct or I for incorrect usage. On the back of this sheet, rewrite any incorrect sentences so they are correct.
  _____ 1. The Mormons' *trek* through the wilderness led them to Utah and the freedom to worship as they wished.
  _____ 2. A *conflagration* broke out between members of the opposing teams.
  _____ 3. The requirements for club membership are very *stringent*; almost anyone can join.
  _____ 4. A car with its windows rolled up can be like an *inferno* on a hot, sunny day for a pet left waiting inside.
  _____ 5. The remote island is a *refuge* for birds seeking quiet, undisturbed nesting places.

C. Choose one.
  1. A few months after the fire, a newspaper headline read, "Chicago: The Phoenix City." Research the legend of the phoenix.
  2. Another great city of wood burned in A.D. 64—Rome. Read to learn about the emperor Nero and the role Christianity played in this fire.
  3. Personification is a figure of speech in which a nonliving thing is described as if it were a person. Use personification and write what the people of Chicago might have said about the fire that burned their city and the rain that put it out.

A Deadly Game

Name _____

Ring-a-ring of rosies, pocket full of posies,
A-tishoo! A-tishoo! We all fall down!

Believe it or not, this innocent circle game is about a disease. The familiar old rhyme makes fun of the plague, also called *Black Death*, which killed more than one fourth of the population of Europe in the 1300s. Today, we know what causes the plague and how to control it. But earlier cultures had no defense against the horrible illness other than to make fun of it.

Certain species of rats carry the germs that cause plague. Fleas transmit the disease to humans, especially those living in crowded, unsanitary areas. The nursery rhyme describes the deadly symptoms: first a tell-tale red rash appears in ring formation on the skin, followed by sneezing ("A-tishoo!") and physical collapse. The disease kills quickly. A victim who appears to be healthy one day can fall down dead the next. A plague epidemic in Rome in A.D. 262 killed 5,000 people a day. The disease spread to Europe, claiming victims in Russia, Italy, France, Germany, and England. In 1894 ships from Hong Kong carried plague-infested rats to India, where more than 10 million people died from the disease over the next 20 years.

Children today still sing the rhyme written about this disease, and governments still watch it carefully. A vaccine and antibodies have been developed that help, but outbreaks can occur anywhere rats hide in cargo ships or trains. Even nations that are political enemies join together in fighting this terrible killer.

A. Many other well-known nursery rhymes grew out of actual events. For each rhyme below, write the letter of the matching fact.

_____ 1. Rock-a-bye, Baby
_____ 2. Jack and Jill
_____ 3. Jack Be Nimble
_____ 4. Little Jack Horner
_____ 5. Sing a Song of Sixpence

  a. Tells of an old-fashioned way of predicting the future: hopping over a burning candle.
  b. Comes from a favorite recipe of the sixteenth century: baking live birds between two crusts.
  c. Originally told of two men, Jack and Gill, ambassadors who held peace talks but stumbled and failed.
  d. Comes from an actual pie stuffed with ownership papers to 12 mansions, sent as a Christmas gift to the king of England. The messenger supposedly reached into the pie to take one of the mansions for himself.
  e. Believed to have been written by a traveler on the *Mayflower* who saw Indian mothers hang their babies from trees in bark cradles.

B. Create your own nursery rhyme about an event currently making news headlines.

Name _____

Atomic Nightmare

In a split-second, fireball blast, almost five square miles of the city of Hiroshima exploded on August 6, 1945. Three days later, another man-made explosion destroyed parts of Nagasaki. It was only after lengthy introspection that U.S. President Harry S Truman ordered the dropping of nuclear bombs on Japan. The newly developed secret weapons promised mass destruction; what no one knew for certain was the degree of devastation. The bombing decisively ended World War II, but its horrible aftermath changed forever attitudes about war.

In both cities, the intense heat of the blast wave almost immediately vaporized anyone within three miles of ground zero. Experts estimate that nearly 4,000 people in Hiroshima died this way. They were the lucky ones, for another large segment of the population, living within six miles of the blast, suffered burns, internal injuries, and intense pain before dying in the days and weeks that followed. But there was a third category of victims, those who escaped immediate death but nevertheless were exposed to massive amounts of radiation. Initially, they suffered extreme nausea and lost their hair. Much worse were the deadly cancers that developed later, as cells altered by the radiation grew in their bodies. Equally horrible were the genetic defects that showed up in their children, born years after the bombs fell. As the world wept with those suffering in Hiroshima and Nagasaki, it became very clear that peace through negotiation and disarmament was mankind's only defense against atomic annihilation.

A. Research to learn the pros and cons of nuclear power.
   1. What happened at Bikini Atoll, Three Mile Island, and Chernobyl?
   2. What positive uses does radiation have in medicine, communications, industry, and scientific research?

B. On the back of this sheet, answer the questions below containing vocabulary words from the selection.
   1. To what topic have you devoted a great deal of *introspection?* Why?
   2. Which *segment* of an Oreo cookie is your favorite? Why?
   3. Does your family prefer *negotiation* over open conflict? Explain.
   4. Come up with a *disarmament* plan that would appeal to violent gang members.
   5. If you could choose one segment of the insect kingdom for *annihilation*, what would it be and why?

C. In deciding to drop the bomb, President Truman held the lives of thousands of people in his hands. Could you handle that kind of pressure? What thoughts, good and bad, might go through your mind? Write your thoughts on the back of this sheet.

D. Make up an acrostic for the one thing nuclear war taught us to want, peace. Write a phrase beginning with each letter.
   P =
   E =
   A =
   C =
   E =

Name _____

The Cat Conundrum

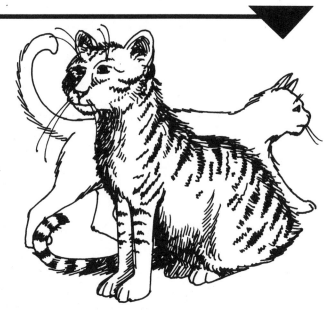

A cat, so old wives say, has nine lives. Cat lovers will tell you the creature has multiple personalities as well: ruthless hunter; alley cat howling at the moon; playful and affectionate pet; aloof loner, regal and independent; or creature of darkness, riding on a witch's broom. Which is the true cat? A look at feline anatomy and human history sheds light on this conundrum.

Cats belong to a world-wide family of meat-eating mammals, *Felidae*. Relatives include panthers, lions, tigers, and leopards. All have long, thin muscles attached to unique joints that allow for great control, balance, and flexibility. Cat watchers have seen something uncanny in the way these creatures move so swiftly and silently, or walk along impossibly narrow ledges, or twist to land on their feet after every fall, or magically extend and retract deadly claws. But there is no supernatural power at work; it is merely a function of the cat's body structure.

Eyes that glow in the dark are another of the cat's attributes that humans find disturbing. This eery shine is due to a mirror-like part at the back of the cat's eye, the *tapetum lucidum*. Light bounces off this structure, enabling the animal to see well in dim light. A cat can stare unblinkingly for long moments before pouncing; does it have hypnotic powers over its prey? Again, the answer comes from anatomy. Unlike most creatures, the cat possesses a third eyelid, located in the inner corner of each eye. This lid provides an extra measure of protection and lubrication, so the cat does not need to blink as frequently as other animals do.

Adding to the cat's aura of mystery are its abilities to pick up on sound and motion unperceivable to human senses. Although the cat cannot see color, it can detect the slightest movement and hears a range of sounds much wider than humans do. But the most sensitive organ on a cat's body is its whiskers. These hairs located on the sides of the face and above the eyes are known as *vibrissae*. Attached to nerves in the skin, they detect vibrations as minute as a slight change in the breeze.

No one knows when humans and felines first began to interact, but records show that domesticated wildcats were used to rid Egyptian granaries of rats and mice as early as 3500 B.C. Because of this important duty, cat worship had spread throughout Asia by 800 B.C. But the tide of public opinion regarding cats turned in the Middle Ages as the more subtle feline traits became associated with witchcraft and superstition. The wholesale destruction of cats was a large factor in the spread of bubonic plague. Unchecked, the rat population exploded, spreading germs of the deadly disease through all of Europe. By the 1600s people once again recognized the value of staying vermin-free, and cats traveled with European colonists all over the globe. Today, people everywhere enjoy cats for attributes they feared or worshiped in centuries past.

Name _____

The Cat Conundrum

A. For each word write the letter of the correct definition.

____ 1. ruthless		a.	a storehouse for grain
____ 2. aloof		b.	any offensive animal
____ 3. feline		c.	mysterious, weird
____ 4. conundrum		d.	indifferent, removed in feeling
____ 5. uncanny		e.	crafty and sly
____ 6. attribute		f.	pertaining to cats, cat-like
____ 7. aura		g.	cruel, without pity
____ 8. granary		h.	a character trait
____ 9. wily		i.	a distinctive atmosphere around a person
____ 10. vermin		j.	a puzzling question

B. Fill in the blanks with vocabulary words.
1. Which came first, the chicken or the egg, is a common _____.
2. Dark organ music playing in the distant tower room added to the castle's _____ of gloom.
3. His tendency to boast is an _____ he was working hard to eradicate.
4. My mother has the _____ ability to know when I am not being entirely truthful.
5. The movie star remained _____ from her eager fans. "Please leave me alone," she said.
6. He was a _____ comedian; no one was safe from his stinging remarks.
7. She shuddered at the thought of living in the _____-infested room.
8. Wheat stored in a _____ emits a gas that can easily ignite.
9. Awakening from her nap, Sherry yawned and stretched with _____ grace.
10. The runner stole second base in a _____ move.

C. Complete this graph to show how the cat's status has changed over the centuries. Make certain you include the five different times mentioned in the selection.

worship	
use and enjoy	
fear	

D. On the back of this sheet, give a definition for each common cat expression below.

1. a cat nap		7.	a cat burglar
2. a cool cat		8.	cattails
3. a copy cat		9.	a scaredy cat
4. cat's cradle		10.	raining cats and dogs
5. a catwalk		11.	fight like cats and dogs
6. the cat's pajamas		12.	let the cat out of the bag

E. Choose one of these cat topics to research.
1. What was the role of the cat in ancient Egyptian religion?
2. How do other members of the cat family compare with the domestic cat?
3. Which well-known fairy tales and nursery rhymes feature cats?

Name _____

Ear to the Ground ⟶ ▼

A robin searching for worms will cock its head to one side and lean toward the ground. A few seconds, pause, a quick stab in the dirt, and it's supper time for the robin. This commonly observed behavior has led people to believe that birds can hear worms moving underground. Since there are no ears visible on a bird's head, ornithologists wanted to know if this assumption was true.

To find out, they had to take one common avian feature into account. Unlike humans, the eyes of most birds are positioned on the sides of their heads. This means that in order to see an object out in front, birds must turn their heads to look with one eye or the other, in what is known as monocular vision. (Humans' vision is binocular; both eyes see the same view at one time.) It was possible, experts reasoned, that a bird was simply examining the ground for disturbed dirt, the sure sign of a worm burrowing below. To rule out this possibility, tests were conducted in which birds were blindfolded. Even without their ability to see, the birds still followed the familiar pattern of cocking their heads and leaning forward. Deprived of sight, they were just as successful in locating worms. That led scientists to conclude that the old folk wisdom was right. The birds were aiming the feather-covered opening to the inner ear toward the ground. Even without external ears, their hearing was keen enough to detect the faint wiggle of dinner underground. The early bird, you see, always catches the noisy worm.

A. Circle the best summary sentence for this passage.
1. Scientists proved that birds see with one eye at a time.
2. Scientists proved folk wisdom that birds can hear worms underground.
3. Birds lack external ears.
4. Old folk wisdom claimed that birds could hear worms.
5. Birds have keen senses of sight and hearing.

B. The word *avian* in the selection above is an animal adjective. It describes anything pertaining to birds. There is a long list of similar adjectives describing other animals. For each word below, give the correct beast.
1. apian _____
2. aquiline _____
3. bovine _____
4. canine _____
5. equine _____
6. feline _____
7. piscine _____
8. porcine _____
9. simian _____
10. ursine _____

C. Ornithology is the scientific study of birds. Research one of the individuals below to learn his contribution to ornithology.
1. Icarus
2. John James Audubon
3. Roger Tory Peterson

Name _____

Sea Skimmers

Many an ocean voyager has laughed with delight at the first glimpse of one of nature's most joyous creatures, the flying fish. Without warning, schools of these small fish explode out of the tropical sea to skim over the waves, sometimes traveling as much as 150 feet before dropping back down underwater. The secret to the fishes' flight lies in specialized fin and tail action.

Strong body muscles give the tail an extra powerful flip to propel the flying fish into the air. Then oversized front fins unfold and spread out stiffly on either side. Vibrating these fins as swiftly as a bird beats its wings, the fish moves forward. If the wind happens to be blowing in the same direction, it gives the flying fish an extra push. After a few seconds' glide, the weight of the fish begins to overcome the lift of its fluttering fins, and the fish begins to drop, tail-first, closer to the water. The instant the tail breaks the surface, the fish gives another powerful flip and pushes itself back up again for more furious fluttering. In this manner, the flying fish can cover long distances, skipping up and down like a stone tossed across a pond.

Why do the fish fly? The most obvious reasons do not answer the question completely. Most fish swim to locate new sources of food or to escape from an enemy. But schools of flying fish take to the air shortly after eating and when there are no predators in sight. Could it be, like man, they sometimes fly just for the thrill of it?

A. Write T for true or F for false.

_____ 1. The flying fish depends entirely on wing-like fins to fly.
_____ 2. When flying fish are active, you can be certain there are enemies nearby.
_____ 3. Flying fish are found in warm waters.
_____ 4. Like a diver, the flying fish reenters the water headfirst.
_____ 5. Catching the wind can prolong the fish's flight.
_____ 6. The fish usually fly in groups.
_____ 7. The fish uses its wings to lift itself out of the water.
_____ 8. The flying fish sails across the water in a long, unbroken path.

B. Alliteration is the repetition of initial sounds in a phrase or sentence. It delights the reader's ear and captures the essence of the subject it describes. On the back of this sheet, write three alliterative sentences about flying fish. Here is a sample: Flipping, flopping, flashing, the flying fish flickered as he flew across our net.

Name _____

The Garish Gar

Pickled pigs' feet, mashed turnips, raw oysters, and tofu—the diversity of foods that human beings will consume is mind-boggling. And as world population soars and food options shrink, man's omnivorous nature is more important than ever. But in spite of dwindling resources, there is one food most people will not eat simply because of color—the marine gar. The gar is a large, slender fish plentiful in the salt waters of the East Coast, from Canada to Mexico. Its body is covered with hard, tan-colored scales, and it bears a long bill equipped with sharp teeth. Because the gar is a fast swimmer and a fierce hunter, its flesh is firm, lean, and can be tasty when cooked, much like mackerel. Yet most people will not consider gar a suitable dish for dinner because of its bones. For some strange reason yet to be discovered, the gar's skeleton is always bright green. It remains that way no matter what culinary efforts are exerted to render the fish more palatable. Somehow, the sight of a neon spine intersecting tender, white meat serves as an instant appetite suppressant; most fishermen throw the gar they catch back into the water in disgust. Scientists and food experts are currently studying the gar to determine the reason for the shocking colored bones. Until they solve the mystery and can put consumers' minds at ease, the marine gar does not have to worry about finding itself on America's dinner plate!

A. Write T for true or F for false.
    _____ 1. Human beings can safely eat foods derived from both plants and animals.
    _____ 2. Lengthy boiling will bleach the color from the gar's bones.
    _____ 3. As natural resources shrink, man's food choices increase.
    _____ 4. The gar's body contains large pockets of fat.
    _____ 5. The meat of the gar is edible.
    _____ 6. Despite its color, fishermen put the gar to good use.

B. A glowing green skeleton can provide the backbone for a good science fiction story. Choose one of the titles below or create your own. Make certain that your story explains the reason for the unusual color of the gar's bones.
    1. Dr. Fizzo's Fiendish Fish
    2. The Fish Files
    3. Bone Zone
    4. Gar from a Far Star

C. Good chefs know, taste alone will not make a feast. Use examples to explain the importance of visual appeal in creating a meal that satisfies.

D. Plan a Gross Feast of ten utterly disgusting foods. Create a menu for your party, complete with detailed descriptions and illustrations. Will you serve gar?

Name _____

Scorpion Secret ──────────────────▼

At first glance, the scorpion looks like a demented doodle that leaped to life from an artist's pen. Its features come straight out of a nightmare: pinchers and claws to crush prey, 6 to 12 eyes, spider-like legs for creeping into dark corners, and, worst of all, a segmented tail that whips forward to inflict a deadly sting. But the scorpion is actually a masterpiece of design, with features that stand up to an austere environment.

Scorpions have been around since the first creatures walked on the earth. Fossil evidence reveals that they have changed little over the eons. All 700 species found worldwide have eight legs, making them members of the Arachnid family along with spiders and ticks. Their hard, shiny, external shell provides protection and enables them to thrive in arid climates. Unlike skin with pores, this exoskeleton cuts down on the loss of body fluids when temperatures soar. All species carry venom in their tails but, for most, the poison only paralyzes prey. The desert scorpions carry the strongest venom, enough to kill a man, another measure that prevents the waste of precious energy in battle. There is one curious characteristic, however, for which science has no explanation. Scorpions' bodies absorb energy in such a way that the animals become fluorescent when exposed to ultraviolet rays. This makes them easily spotted at night by anyone shining a black light. Until scientists understand this odd capability, it will only serve to heighten our morbid fascination with the scorpion.

A. For each word write the letter of the correct definition.

- _____ 1. demented   a. dry, barren
- _____ 2. eons   b. severe, harsh
- _____ 3. arid   c. insane
- _____ 4. morbid   d. gruesome
- _____ 5. austere   e. an immeasurably long time period

B. Match these vocabulary riddles with the correct answers.

- _____ 1. An austere swamp is . . . .
- _____ 2. An arid seventh month is . . . .
- _____ 3. Glowing color that lasts a long time is . . . .
- _____ 4. Morbid twins are . . . .
- _____ 5. A demented flower is . . . .

a. neon for the eons   d. the gruesome twosome
b. a crazy daisy   e. a dry July
c. a harsh marsh

C. Nature is practical; almost nothing exists in the world that does not serve a function or fill a need. On the back of this sheet, suggest five possibilities for scorpions' fluorescence.

D. Over 2,000 years ago, people looking at the night sky saw a cluster of stars that resembled a scorpion. They believed that individuals born when the sun traveled near this constellation would have certain characteristics. Research to learn more about the scorpion sign of the zodiac.

Name _____

A Tail Tale

How and why animals got their tails is a favorite subject for stories from many different cultures. But a survey of true-life tails makes for a tale all the more fascinating because it is factual. In their various shapes and sizes, tails serve as decoys and lures, defensive weapons, signaling devices, propellers and brakes, balance beams, blankets, and storehouses for fat reserves.

It is underwater that tails are perhaps the most necessary, being the primary means of locomotion and steering for thousands of species of fish. The side-to-side movement of body and tail propels most fish forward through the water. The tadpole has nothing on which to rely other than the wiggle of its hind end. The seahorse straightens its tail to rise and curls it to sink; the flip of a crayfish tail achieves swift backward movement. Land creatures also depend on their tails for travel—the pallid gerbil's exceptionally long tail provides balance and stability in running and jumping; the eagle's tail fans to slow its rapid flight enough to allow for a landing. For kangaroos, the long, stiff tail serves as a fifth leg, providing additional lift for those long jumps. Woodpeckers, monkeys, and chameleons all rely on their tails to cling securely to their treetop perches.

Anyone familiar with domesticated animals has read the language of the tail; creatures in the wild exhibit the same signals. A lashing tail indicates anger, whether it belongs to a panther or a frilled lizard. Gentle twitching, on the other hand, means concentration or contentment. Purposeful twitching shoos away flies, and the unfurled tail, as in the peacock's display, means, "Hello, ladies!" Some tails are designed to distract. The Indian moon moth's long tail dangles inches beneath the creature's leafy hiding place, luring predators away from its soft head and body. The dark tuft punctuating a lion's tail also serves to confound would-be attackers. Which is the head and which is the tail? Is there one lion or two?

Still other tails are equipped for defense or protection—both scorpions and sting rays carry poison in their hindmost parts. The tree skink and the glass lizard shed their tails in a pinch. Muscles along the spine contract sharply when these tails are grasped, causing bones at the end to crack off. Fortunately, new bones eventually grow back. The Arctic fox uses its tail as protection from its frigid environment, wrapping the thick fur around itself like a blanket. The tails of the dab lizard and some breeds of sheep thicken and swell with stored food during times of abundance, so nourishment will be available when food is sparse.

Given its range of usefulness in the animal kingdom, the tail is in no danger of becoming obsolete. Instead, it poses an interesting question: since the tail is such a serviceable part, why is it missing from the human anatomy?

A Tail Tale

Name _____

A. For each word write the letter of the correct definition.

_____ 1. decoy   a. to throw into confusion
_____ 2. locomotion   b. a cluster or clump
_____ 3. pallid   c. no longer in use
_____ 4. lashing   d. a great plenty
_____ 5. unfurled   e. movement from place to place
_____ 6. tuft   f. a lure, bait
_____ 7. punctuate   g. having few in number
_____ 8. confound   h. striking quickly
_____ 9. abundance   i. lacking in color
_____ 10. sparse   j. unfolded
_____ 11. obsolete   k. to stop or emphasize

B. Mark each sentence below C for correct or I for incorrect vocabulary usage.

_____ 1. The toddler was *obsolete* about not taking her nap.
_____ 2. A nail *punctuated* my tire on the drive home.
_____ 3. Steam-powered *locomotion* ended the era of the horse-drawn carriage.
_____ 4. A haircut was always a lengthy ordeal due to his *sparse* head of hair.
_____ 5. This heavy rain means we will have an *abundance* of mushrooms in a day or so.
_____ 6. A tongue *lashing* can sometimes inflict more pain than a spanking.
_____ 7. We climbed to the *tuft* of the hill.
_____ 8. Deep purple clouds and a bright orange sun made for a *pallid* scene.
_____ 9. We floated *decoys* on the pond to attract wild ducks.
_____ 10. At three days, the kittens' eyes were still *unfurled*.
_____ 11. The riddle *confounded* all the king's wise men.

C. For each I above, write a correct sentence on the back of this sheet.

D. For each paragraph in this reading selection find the correct topic heading from the list below. Label I, II, III, IV, and V; you will have leftovers.

_____ 1. Evolution of the tail   _____ 5. Communicating and luring
_____ 2. Question of humans having tails   _____ 6. Defending and protecting
_____ 3. Various purposes of animals' tails   _____ 7. Moving and clinging
_____ 4. Shedding and contracting

E. For each detail below, give the animal or animals mentioned in the selection.
1. Uses tail to attract females   6. Straightens tail to move upward
2. Uses tail as a brake   7. Uses tail for warmth
3. Has detachable tail   8. Lashes tail
4. Uses tail for storage   9. Uses tail to confuse enemies
5. Grasps with tail

Name _____

Unlikely Mermaids

When Ulysses, hero of the ancient Greek poem the *Odyssey*, neared the rocky island of the Sirens, he ordered his sailors to stop up their ears with wax. In this way, none of them would be lured ashore by the ladies' lovely singing. From this ancient story grew the myth of the mermaids, beautiful creatures who were half women and half fish. Lonely mariners far from home believed that mermaids sat combing their long, golden hair and singing as they waited for ships to approach. The creatures would then capture mortal men to live with them under the sea. Centuries later, explorers traveling in tropical regions caught glimpses of plump creatures sunning in shallow water. From a distance, they must have looked a little like humans. Remembering the story of Ulysses' beautiful, half-human mermaids, the sailors named the strange creatures sirens. Had the men taken a closer look, however, they might have chosen another name, for the sirens are surely some of the homeliest animals living today.

Just two species currently survive, the manatee and the dugong. Both can grow up to 13 feet long and weigh hundreds of pounds. They have rounded heads with tiny eyes atop blotchy gray, blimp-shaped bodies scattered with bristles. Their front legs are shaped like flat paddles and their thick, round tails serve as rudders. They have no hind legs. Despite their lack of physical beauty, the creatures move with a slow, gentle grace. They are among the few mammals who live out their entire lives in water, the manatee in the shallow bays and rivers feeding into the Atlantic, and the dugong in the Indian and Pacific Oceans. Placid and lacking any means of self-defense, they contentedly and methodically munch more than 100 pounds of water plants each day. In fact, the people in the South American country of Guyana depend on manatees to keep their waterways free of choking weeds.

Over the centuries, these gentle giants have been easy targets for sailors hunting meat and hides, and several of their kind are now extinct. Today, the creatures' love of warm, shallow water puts them in the path of recreational boaters. Propeller wounds disfigure most of the animals and have caused countless, unnecessary deaths. Pollution and coastal development also compromise their natural grazing areas. Because of rapidly dwindling numbers of manatees and dugongs, scientists have placed them on the list of endangered species. Communities in coastal Florida take pride in their unique marine residents. They tag and protect the few young that are born in their waters and seek to educate boaters who frequent manatee areas.

Despite their association with the legend of Ulysses, neither the manatee nor the dugong has been known to sing. These unlikely mermaids are content with the simple pleasures of eating and basking in the sun. If they send a message to busy human beings, it is this: "Slow down . . . Life is good . . . Enjoy . . . !"

Unlikely Mermaids

Name _____

A. What happened first? Number the events in order from 1 to 5.

_____ 1. Sailors killed off some types of sirens for food.

_____ 2. The myth of the sirens gave birth to a belief in mermaids.

_____ 3. Manatees are threatened by boaters who frequent the same shallow waters.

_____ 4. Sailors who saw distant manatees thought they were mermaids.

_____ 5. Singing sea nymphs named *sirens* tried to lure Ulysses and his men to their dangerous rocks.

B. Each sentence below makes a statement about sirenians that is not entirely true. On the back of this sheet, rewrite the sentences so they do not mislead.

1. Humans should avoid all contact with manatees.

2. Sirenians were safe from humans in the days before motorized boating became popular.

3. There is nothing about the manatee that humans find appealing or useful.

4. Building in coastal areas should be forbidden in order to protect manatee waters.

C. M is for Manatee! Complete each of these M activities.

1. If manatees could sing, what would they say? Write a manatee melody, putting new words to a familiar tune.

2. The Stellar's sea cow is a sirenian we will never see because it became extinct more than 200 years ago. How do the remaining sirenians feel about the loss of their cousin? Write a manatee memorial.

3. Research to create a manatee map showing current habitats.

4. Write five jokes or riddles about the merry manatee. Here are some samples to get you started: What gentle ocean mammal eats 100 pounds of water plants a day and tells jokes? The mana-tee-hee-hee. What do you call a sirenian who kids his friends all the time? A mana-tease. What's gray and weighs 300 pounds? A manatee on a diet.

5. Manatees matter! Create an effective TV commercial to alert the public to the plight of this gentle creature.

D. A baby sirenian is called a calf. A dictionary will help you correctly identify each animal below.

1. a poult _____ 8. a gosling _____

2. a cygnet _____ 9. a leveret _____

3. a kit _____ 10. a fledgling _____

4. a kid _____ 11. a joey _____

5. a fry _____ 12. a squab _____

6. a shoat _____ 13. an elver _____

7. an eyas _____ 14. a spat _____

Name _____

Man's Best Friends

According to the Book of Genesis, man's first job was in management. He was to subdue the earth, to rule over the creatures living in it, to cultivate, to tame, to use and not destroy. Although man has had many, many years to accomplish this task, he has enjoyed only marginal success. Some of the world's animals are extinct, thanks to man, and others live in wild habitats that are on the wane. But in a few significant cases, a mutual dependency exists in which humans and animals look to each other for support and survival. These special animals are truly man's friends.

The cow that gives milk, the sheep whose wool clothes our backs, and the horse that provides transportation immediately come to mind. But there are other services that animals perform in return for their care and feeding. For centuries, Japanese fisherman have kept cormorants, long-necked birds similar to pelicans. The cormorant dives to scoop up fish for his master; a string tied firmly around the bird's neck prevents it from swallowing the fish. In ancient Egypt, herds of pigs were driven across fields to prepare them for planting. As the pigs nosed around, they broke up clods. Their hoofprints made holes the right size for seeds, and they even added their own fertilizer. Southern plantations depended on geese to rid cotton and strawberry fields of weeds, while sheep kept the large, green lawns neatly cropped. In France, modern-day lovers of fine food rely on pigs' discriminating noses to sniff out the underground fungi known as truffles. Over the years, people have domesticated other animals as well: dogs, llamas, camels, elephants, water buffalo, and dolphins. In return for the service these animals perform, man offers protection, food, and attention.

Could these creatures who have grown accustomed to serving man survive without him? Some certainly could. Domestic horses and camels returned to the wild have thrived and multiplied on their own. Some abandoned farm animals have reverted to the behavior of their wild ancestors. But those domestic creatures that have developed special traits over many generations would have much more difficulty making it on their own. How would a cow accustomed to regular milking survive? Could a fragile toy poodle hold its own in a dog-eat-dog world? Serving man impacts many species so much, they could never return to life in the wild.

Of all the creatures that benefit from a relationship with humans, most do not experience friendship with them. Minks, for example, receive much care and attention from their breeders, but never respond in like manner. Totally dependent on man, nevertheless they remain wild at heart.

People enjoy raising baby chicks and tending iguanas—until they become too large to manage easily. To be man's best friend, his pet, an animal must be tolerant of people, gentle enough to handle, relatively easy to feed and care for, and responsive. More than any other service or product an animal provides, man values most the love he receives from his pets.

Man's Best Friends

Name _____

A. For each word write the letter of the correct definition.

_____	1. subdue	a. careful of differences, picky
_____	2. marginal	b. to collide so as to change
_____	3. wane	c. close to the lower level of acceptability
_____	4. clod	d. forsaken, given up
_____	5. crop	e. to overcome in order to control
_____	6. discriminating	f. a lump of earth
_____	7. domesticate	g. to go back to a former state
_____	8. abandoned	h. to decrease
_____	9. revert	i. to cut off short
_____	10. impact	j. to make useful for humans

B. Answer these vocabulary questions on the back of this sheet.
1. Use a calendar to determine if the moon is currently waxing or *waning*. Explain.
2. Design and sketch a creative new *cropped* hairstyle.
3. In old age, some people can *revert* to a second childhood. Explain with examples.
4. Which course at this school has most *impacted* your life and why?
5. What does a *discriminating* shopper do? Are you one? Explain.
6. Explain the reason this book is a best-seller: Ten Easy Steps to a *Domesticated* Husband.
7. What *marginal* behavior have you exhibited lately that your parents have kindly ignored?
8. List five items commonly abandoned in the halls of your school.
9. To whom are *clods* a problem? List three individuals and explain.
10. Suggest five ways a furious person can *subdue* his or her anger.

C. For each detail below, supply the letter of the matching animal. You may use a letter more than once.

_____	1. Weed fields	a. Minks
_____	2. Provide wool	b. Cormorants
_____	3. Can grow too large to manage easily	c. Geese
_____	4. Locate truffles	d. Cows
_____	5. Dive for fish	e. Pigs
_____	6. Provide milk	f. Iguanas
_____	7. Mow grass	g. Sheep
_____	8. Prepare fields	
_____	9. Refuse efforts to tame	
_____	10. Could not survive abandonment	

Name _____

Animal Metropolis

During the early years of the twentieth century, a remarkable town sprang to life in the state of Texas. It covered an area of land roughly 100 by 240 miles and provided shelter for more than 400 million residents. The town's rapid growth was due to its many attractive features: fresh air, well-guarded entrances, comfortable living quarters, manicured landscaping, convenient fast food, effective security measures, even well-equipped nurseries for the infants. Despite its huge population, town living was a pleasure—for the black-tipped prairie dogs that lived in the enormous colony.

While this prairie dog town is the largest on record, it is by no means unusual. Visitors to America's grasslands are fascinated by these small, social rodents who stand on hind legs to yip at passersby, then vanish into extensive burrows underground. Members of an extended family live in a network of individual homes connected by tunnels and large chambers. Here they groom each other, kiss by touching noses, nurse their young, and chatter incessantly. Sentries stand guard, to bark an alarm if predators such as coyotes or eagles approach. When the animals are not foraging for grass and insects to eat, they maintain their town, sealing off soiled burrows, digging new ones, keeping dirt mounded up around entrances, cutting back any weeds that might interfere with their view of the prairie. Because of this industrious nature, prairie dogs never outgrow their colony. They simply continue to enlarge it until some external factor forces family units to break up and start over: a shortage of food, encroaching development, or an increase in enemy presence. As our human cities grow in size, we could learn some lessons from these most successful city-builders of the animal kingdom.

A. Compare human cities to the prairie dog town described in this selection.
   1. How does the population of the prairie dog town compare with that of New York City? Chicago? Los Angeles? Your state capital? The town where your school is located?
   2. Explain five reasons why both prairie dogs and humans like city living.
   3. What factors cause cities to stop growing? Include both human cities and prairie dog towns in your answer.

B. Answer these questions to learn more about the prairie dog's habitat.
   1. Grasslands are located all over the world, but each culture calls them by a different name. For each type of grassland listed, give its location.
      a. pampas _____   d. veldt _____
      b. prairie _____   e. steppe _____
      c. llanos _____

   2. Animals that inhabit the grasslands fall into two categories: the runners (lion, bison, wild horse, kangaroo) and the burrowers (prairie dogs, vizcachas, susliks). How is each type of animal especially well-suited to life on the prairie? Write your thoughts on the back of this sheet.

C. As space on the earth's surface becomes crowded or damaged by pollution, scientists believe man will begin building cities underground. Map out on paper your ideal underground town. Include every feature necessary for a comfortable life.

Name _____

nature's Bristle Balls ➤

Although porcupines have always been unpopular with humans because of sharp and pain-causing quills, they are actually benign animals when left alone. Initially, the quills of a porcupine are soft and silky. Weeks after birth, yellowish-white tips begin to form and thicken. These quills eventually grow as long as seven inches.

When a porcupine feels threatened, it responds by rolling up into a ball of bristles. Most people mistakenly believe that porcupines have the ability to shoot their quills. The truth is that the quills of a porcupine are only loosely fastened to its body and have a tendency to fall out. Quills that fly off a porcupine's swinging tail into the face of an enemy appear to have been shot. In certain types of porcupines, quill tips are covered with barbs which hook into an attacker's flesh. Victims of the porcupine often perish from infected wounds or damage to their vital organs. If quills pierce the area around a victim's mouth, it is often unable to move its jaw and dies of starvation.

Porcupines' true victims are not people or animals, but trees. Using their long, sharp claws to climb trunks, porcupines rest on branches and feast on bark and twigs. This causes great damage to forests. In fact, one porcupine can kill up to a hundred trees in the winter months. Porcupines also crave salt. The creatures have been known to sneak into campsites in search of something salty to taste, even nibbling at the sweat on sleeping campers' hands. So the next time you are snacking on your salty popcorn or French fries, look out for porcupines!

A. Write T for true or F for false.

    _____ 1. Porcupines eat small rodents such as rats and mice.

    _____ 2. Porcupines are born with sharp-pointed quills.

    _____ 3. When a porcupine is attacked, it rolls into a ball.

    _____ 4. The quills of a porcupine are so loose, they often fall out.

    _____ 5. Most victims of porcupines die from suffocation.

    _____ 6. The porcupine is a mean and dangerous animal to encounter.

    _____ 7. The real victims of the porcupine are salt distributors.

    _____ 8. A single porcupine can kill a hundred trees in one winter.

    _____ 9. Certain porcupines have barbs which pierce their victims' skin.

    _____ 10. The quills of a porcupine can grow up to seven inches long.

B. Porcupines have unjustly gained a bad reputation due to their sharp quills. For each animal listed below, research and explain the reason for the bad publicity it receives.
1. Komodo dragon   2. skunk
3. opossum   4. rat
5. Rottweiler   6. snake

C. Imagine the surprise finding a porcupine digging through your campground would create! Write a short story in which a porcupine searching for salt is discovered by dismayed campers.

Name _____

Here's to Ears!

Most living creatures have some type of organ that detects sound, but not all creatures have ears. Insects have membranes on their legs that vibrate when sound waves hit them. Fish and snakes only have inner ears and detect sound through their bodies. The eardrum of a frog is the large, flat disc behind each eye, and birds have auditory canals that open directly on the sides of their heads. Of all living creatures, only mammals have the outer fleshy curve of cartilage that scientists call auricles.

These auricles, or ears, are fascinating structures. A lop rabbit's auricles can grow as long as 30 inches. Those of elephants are the largest of all, measuring up to four feet wide. Average human ears can vary from two to six inches. Each is held in place by three tiny muscles. In most mammals, these muscles are well-developed and allow the animal to turn its ears in different directions to receive sound. Only the rare human, however, has enough control of these muscles to wiggle his or her ears. And perhaps that is for the best, since many humans use the lower portion of the ear, the lobe made of loosely hanging fat, to display one or more articles of jewelry.

In their work of funneling sound and flaunting wealth, auricles naturally catch dust. Fortunately, the structure connected with the outer ear, the auditory canal, is a curving tube lined with hair and glands that produce wax. Any dirt particles attracted to the auricle get trapped in earwax before they can move into the inner ear. Occasionally, both humans and animals need assistance in removing the earwax that can build up in the auditory canal.

The design of the inner ear also distinguishes mammals from other creatures. Only mammals have tightly coiled cochleas. While this structure provides for acute hearing, it also makes mammals vulnerable to motion sickness. That is because small mineral grains embedded in the inner ear react to gravity. If you and your dog get in an elevator and descend rapidly, both of you will feel discomfort in your ears. You might even notice that your hearing is impaired during the trip. On the other hand, a bird that swoops down from its mountaintop perch rarely experiences such difficulty. Mammalian ears seem to be distinctly designed for a sedentary life, while other creatures' ears can better handle the changes in pressure, gravity, and movement that characterize their instinctual behavior.

Here's to Ears!

Name _____

A. Use vocabulary words from the selection to correctly fill in the blanks in these sentences.

auditory	cartilage
flaunt	acute
vulnerable	impair
sedentary	instinctual

1. Prior to his heart attack, my father felt _____ pain in his chest and arms.

2. A wise man does not _____ his wealth.

3. Emily Dickinson lived a _____ life, rarely stepping foot outside her own house.

4. If you are having trouble with homework, clear away any distractions that might _____ your ability to concentrate.

5. She is an _____ learner; she learns best by listening carefully.

6. Parenthood is not _____; most of us learn how to be good mothers and fathers in the school of experience.

7. _____ is more elastic than bone, but it still may be crushed by a hard blow.

8. All alone down by the goal, the soccer player was _____ to any move the opposing team might make.

B. On a separate sheet of paper, draw a diagram of an ear, inner and outer. Label your drawing with the facts provided in this selection.

C. Write T for true or F for false.

____ 1. Elephants have auditory canals.

____ 2. Auricles are a combination of bone, muscle, cartilage, and fat.

____ 3. Some creatures other than mammals may have cochleas, just not tightly coiled ones.

____ 4. Fish have muscles that allow them to move their auricles.

____ 5. Space travel, with its zero gravity, affects human hearing.

____ 6. Frogs produce earwax.

D. Appreciate your auricles! On the back of this sheet, list five sounds that you especially love to hear and explain why.

E. This selection was written as if the reader was unfamiliar with ears. Write a description that would help an extraterrestrial reader understand toes. _____
_____
_____

Name _____

Whose Shoes?

It is vacation, and you get up early to be first out on the beach. But when you cross the dunes, it appears that a crowd has beaten you there, for tiny, white bedroom shoes lie scattered up and down the water's edge. They are the discarded shells of the Atlantic slipper, a snail-like animal common to our Eastern shores.

About two inches long, each oval shell has a shelf covering one-third of the opening, making it look just like a slip-on shoe. The animal who creates this interesting shell spends its early life in shallow water searching for a home base. Finally it attaches itself to any hard surface: a rock, a horseshoe crab, even another Atlantic slipper. To feed, it filters plankton from the water. But most curious of all is that the slipper is hermaphroditic, capable of functioning as both male and female. When the animal is young and roaming, it is usually male. As the creature matures and settles on a surface, its female parts become active.

A. Circle the best title.
    1. East Coast Shellfish
    2. A Plankton Feeder
    3. She Sells Seashell Shoes
    4. The Atlantic Slipper
    5. Hermaphroditism

B. Write T for true or F for false.
    _____ 1. The Atlantic slipper has both male and female organs.
    _____ 2. Young children enjoy wearing the shells on their feet.
    _____ 3. Young female slippers travel across the ocean floor depositing their eggs.
    _____ 4. Beachcombers can sometimes find colonies of slippers attached one on top of another.
    _____ 5. Male slippers are young and restless.
    _____ 6. Beachcombers travel to both Atlantic and Pacific coasts to find slipper shells.

C. Read to find out more. Write your findings on another sheet of paper.
    1. In Greek mythology, who was Hermaphroditus?
    2. What is unique about the sailing vessel known as a hermaphrodite brig? Draw a diagram and explain.
    3. How is the hermaphroditism of the common earthworm different from that of the Atlantic slipper?
    4. What other seashells are named for their close resemblance to common objects? Draw sketches and explain.

D. Imagine and write a story about a race of tiny people who use Atlantic slipper shells as shoes, boats, or cradles.

Unbelievable Bezoars

Name _____

Bezoars are up at the top of nature's list of oddities. These smooth, shiny spheres can range from golf ball to baseball size. Surprisingly lightweight, they reveal dry, matted hair very much like felt when cut open. Bezoars, or hair balls, occasionally develop in the stomachs of ruminant animals such as cows, deer, buffalo, or llamas. When these creatures lick and groom themselves, the hair they swallow can collect in the stomach. Over time, body fluids form a hard coating around the clump, similar to an eggshell. Called concretion, it is the same process that produces pearls in oysters and gallstones in human beings.

The ancient Persians believed that bezoars had miraculous restorative powers. Any bezoars found in the bodies of slaughtered animals were made into goblets, complete with jeweled stems. Physicians prescribed a bezoar of strong elixir for their dying patients. The king himself drank from a bezoar goblet daily, in hopes that the cup would neutralize any toxin an enemy might have slipped into his wine.

A. Use context clues from the selection to define these vocabulary words.

   1. sphere _____

   2. matted _____

   3. ruminant _____

   4. concretion_____

   5. restorative_____

   6. elixir_____

   7. toxin _____

B. Write T for true or F for false.
   _____ 1. Cows regularly cough up bezoars.
   _____ 2. Persians frequently tried to poison their kings.
   _____ 3. The inside of a bezoar is damp and heavy with decay.
   _____ 4. Ruminants cannot digest hair.
   _____ 5. Physicians used bezoar goblets as a last hope for terminally-ill patients.
   _____ 6. Gallstones form in people who swallow hair.

C. Mankind has always attached special significance, value, or power to rare, one-of-a-kind items such as bezoars, unicorns, four-leaf clovers, and antiques. On the back of this sheet, list at least three more examples and explain why people think this way.

D. Choose a title below and write a bezoar mystery on a sheet of notebook paper.
   a. Aladdin's Goblet
   b. The Riddle of the Cup
   c. The Battle of the Bezoar
   d. Drink the Last Drop

Name _____

Friend in the Sea ───────────────────►

Of all the creatures that swim, fly, or crawl the earth, few are friendlier to man than the dolphin. Ever since the first boat ventured out to sea, humans have valued this marine mammal for its playful personality and permanent smile, its non-aggressive behavior, and its uncanny ability to locate large schools of fish. Dolphin drawings dating back as far as 2200 B.C. have been found from the shores of Western Europe to the deserts of the Middle East. Over the centuries, the dolphin has been revered as the harbinger of good weather, the protector of ocean travelers, and the conductor for the dead, providing safe passage to the shores of the next world. Some church historians believe the fish symbol, still in use today, grew in part out of association with the dolphin.

The dolphin has captured modern man's imagination as well, starring in television shows and aquatic acts or gently nudging sick children back to health in medical experiments. When stories of dolphin drownings made the news, the public demanded immediate action. Somersaulting behind fishing fleets, hundreds of friendly dolphins were getting caught in tuna nets. Legislators passed laws that forced the fishing industry to develop more humane practices that spare the dolphin. Even the U.S. Navy likes this intelligent creature and has found ways it can be of service. With a minimum of training, dolphins learn to retrieve underwater objects. In the Vietnam War, a small corps of trained dolphins carried darts designed to puncture and destroy enemy divers' air tanks.

The navy's latest project makes use of the dolphin's sense of echolocation, its unique system of "reading" the sound waves it bounces off of solid objects. The dolphin is armed with an explosive device and released in waters where submarines are hidden. Through echolocation, the dolphin distinguishes between friendly and enemy subs. This is possible because of special metal plates bolted to the sides of American submarines. The sound waves bouncing off these plates are different from the vibrations made by other vessels' sides. Once the dolphin has located an enemy sub, it deposits the mine on the ship's side and swims away to safety.

Scientists will undoubtedly develop new missions for the dolphin as we learn more about its unique capabilities. But each ocean wave that laps the shore whispers a disturbing question. Will modern man use or abuse this talented and friendly creature of the sea?

93

Friend in the Sea

Name _____

A. Circle the best title for the selection.
1. Dolphin Worship
2. Uses for Trained Dolphins
3. Echolocation
4. Man and Dolphins through the Ages
5. The Future of Dolphins

B. Write the topic sentences for paragraphs 1 and 2 on the back of this sheet.

C. Compare the modern fascination with wild creatures such as the dolphin to the ancient world's worship of them. Discuss similarities and differences.

D. Research to answer the following:
1. What are the differences between dolphins and porpoises?
2. What other creatures belong to the dolphin family?
3. What is the myth that connects the Greek god Apollo with an ancient temple at Delphi and dolphins?

E. On another sheet of paper, predict the future for the dolphin. Will it serve mankind or rebel? Will it unlock the secrets of the sea? Will it become extinct? Give reasons for your predictions.

F. For each word write the letter of the correct definition.
_____ 1. venture
_____ 2. aggressive
_____ 3. revere
_____ 4. harbinger
_____ 5. aquatic
_____ 6. lap
_____ 7. humane

a. one who goes before
b. to flow against with a licking sound
c. to dare forward
d. of the water
e. to regard with awe or worship
f. disposed to attack
g. kind

G. Fill in the blanks with the correct vocabulary words.

1. For many people, the first robin is a _____ of spring.

2. _____ behavior belongs on the playing field, not in the classroom.

3. International law requires that all prisoners of war receive _____ treatment.

4. The dog noisily _____ the water from the puddle.

5. Space explorers _____ where no man has gone before.

6. Many people _____ movie stars and professional athletes.

7. _____ sports have long been an official part of the Summer Olympics.

Name _____

Itching to Know ──────────────────▼

Are you itching to know how to avoid painful mosquito bites? Although most bites just itch for a day or two and then heal, some can result in illness and death from malaria, yellow fever, or encephalitis. That is why scientists are working hard to find ways to stop mosquitoes from biting. The solution is much more difficult to achieve than you might realize.

First, it is helpful to understand some basic facts about the mosquito. Only the female bites; she does so to get blood, the one food that will help her produce eggs. The word "bite" is technically incorrect, for the insect actually stabs its victim with six tiny needles at the end of its proboscis, a long, nose-like projection. Saliva from the mosquito's mouth flows down the proboscis into the wound. This saliva causes an allergic reaction in most humans, forming an itchy welt. The mosquito drinks enough blood to distend its abdomen, taking in as much as one and a half times its own weight. It will not sting again until its stomach is empty, as much as 24 hours later.

There are more than 3,000 different species of mosquitoes, and each one seeks out the blood of a different kind of animal. Sensory organs on the female's body are extremely perceptive. A mosquito that needs dog blood will not bite until it finds a dog—even if there are plenty of human targets available. Researchers now believe that mosquitoes can even differentiate between people, preferring to bite certain individuals over others. Folk wisdom claims it is because some people are "sweet"; science says it is due to their metabolism. The mosquitoes that sting humans are attracted by the carbon dioxide released as a body breaks down food into proteins and energy. An individual whose body does this quickly puts off more carbon dioxide than someone with a slower metabolism. That means mosquitoes look for high-energy people to bite.

The fact that mosquitoes are such picky eaters multiplies the problem scientists face in looking for effective repellents. What discourages one type of mosquito from seeking one particular type of blood does not affect the 2,999 other mosquitoes at all. So researchers continue to study these complex insects. In the meantime, the best methods of preventing the spread of mosquito-borne disease have undesirable side effects. Many communities spray chemical insecticides to eliminate mosquitoes. But this poison kills beneficial insects at the same time and can even harm some humans and animals. The other common method of control is to drain the wetlands where most mosquitoes breed. This, too, is costly in the plants and animals it kills.

Maybe you think the answer to the problem is to move to a place where mosquitoes do not live. Unfortunately, you will have to look long and hard, for mosquitoes are found all over the world, even in the Arctic! Until science gets as smart as nature, you will just have to swat and bear it!

Itching to Know

A. For each word write the letter of the correct definition.

_____ 1. projection   a. a substance that drives away

_____ 2. welt   b. the belly

_____ 3. distend   c. a preparation for killing insects

_____ 4. abdomen   d. a raised ridge of flesh

_____ 5. sensory   e. a jutting out

_____ 6. perceptive   f. carried

_____ 7. metabolism   g. to stretch

_____ 8. repellent   h. pertaining to the nerve centers

_____ 9. borne   i. the process by which cells create energy

_____10. insecticide   j. having awareness

B. For each vocabulary word listed above, write an original sentence on the back of this sheet.

C. When you know the -CIDE root, you have a key to an entire family of rather unpleasant words. For each word below, identify the type of killing.

_____ 1. suicide   _____ 6. genocide
_____ 2. parricide   _____ 7. homicide
_____ 3. fratricide   _____ 8. sororicide
_____ 4. matricide   _____ 9. patricide
_____ 5. infanticide   _____10. filicide

D. Circle the best title: Mosquitoes' Life Cycle, Kinds of Mosquitoes, The Buzz on Mosquito Bites, Repelling Mosquitoes, Mosquito-Borne Diseases

E. Write T for true or F for false.

_____ 1. A person with slow metabolism attracts fewer mosquitoes.

_____ 2. The only places that have no mosquitoes are those with very cold climates.

_____ 3. Itchy welts are caused by malaria germs.

_____ 4. Male mosquitoes do not sting.

_____ 5. Current methods of controlling mosquitoes do as much harm as good.

_____ 6. Mosquitoes must fill their stomachs at least three times a day.

_____ 7. Most mosquitoes do not spread deadly diseases.

_____ 8. A mosquito is attracted to blood, no matter what kind it is.

_____ 9. Few people react to mosquito bites.

_____10. Mosquitoes sting people who have sweet-tasting skin.

Name _____

Down and Dirty

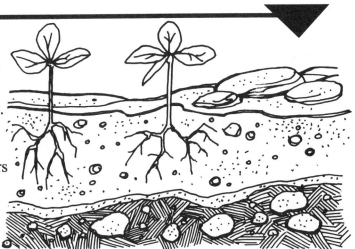

All of us depend on dirt from the moment of our birth until the day that we die. Dirt grows the food we eat and the fibers we weave into clothes. It is a part of the dishes from which we eat. It provides materials and support for the buildings we live in. Kids and athletes play on dirt; mothers fuss when it stains our clothes. The road builder smooths out dirt, the miner tunnels into it, the archaeologist sifts through it for clues about the past. And in the end, dirt accepts our worn-out bodies and makes more dirt from them. For most of human history, we have taken dirt for granted. But in those times when dirt disappears, we realize that it is one of our most precious resources, to be treated with care.

That is what Americans learned during the Dust Bowl disaster of the 1930s, when drought hit what once had been rich prairie grassland. For years, farmers had tilled under the hardy, native grass, cultivating less-sturdy wheat in its place. Their livestock roamed the prairie that remained, nibbling away deeply rooted plants that secured the soil. Without protection, the dirt dried out; then high winds began to blow. In one storm alone, more than 350 million tons of topsoil blew off the fields of Kansas, Oklahoma, and Texas. What had taken centuries for nature to create was gone. Working with experts, farmers learned to protect and slowly rebuild fields from the dirt that was left, but it was a lesson that cost the entire nation much in suffering and economic hardship.

All soil is the product of a complex cycle. It begins as rock weathers and disintegrates into small, mineral-rich particles. Plants and animals living amid these rocks die and decay, adding their nutrients to the mixture. Water and air, time and temperature all work to bind the ingredients into a miracle substance that grows giant sequoia trees, acres of corn, and delicate violets. But that is only one half of the cycle. The very forces that create dirt also destroy it. Over time, sun, wind, and water can rob soil of its nutrients. Every shower of rain that falls washes dirt particles off the land and into the ocean. There, soil settles as sediment, to be slowly pressed over the ages into layers of rock. When pressure from within the earth heaves these rock layers back onto land, the cycle begins anew.

Soil experts called pedologists recognize ten basic types of dirt—red, yellow, black or brown in color, and ranging from fertile to barren. But within these ten categories are hundreds of regional variations. There is chernozem in Russia—a black soil heavy with decomposed plant material that grows bumper crops of grain. The iron-red soil of Hawaii's prolific pineapple fields comes from time-worn volcanoes. When grains of sand collected at the Atlantic coast ages ago and formed the beach, a residue dense with clay was left behind. North Carolina and Kentucky farmers appreciate their stubborn soil that holds just the amount of water tobacco plants need to thrive. The dirt beneath our feet has a fascinating story to tell to those wise enough to look and learn.

Down and Dirty

A. For each word write the letter of the correct definition.

_____ 1. till
_____ 2. drought
_____ 3. hardy
_____ 4. nutrient
_____ 5. sequoia
_____ 6. sediment
_____ 7. heave
_____ 8. prolific
_____ 9. residue
_____ 10. thrive

a. the matter that settles to the bottom
b. to grow vigorously
c. strong, resistant to hardship
d. that which remains
e. to plow
f. fruitful
g. a healthy ingredient
h. a huge fir tree native to California
i. a long, dry spell
j. to lift or raise

B. For each word pair below, choose S for Synonyms or A for Antonyms.

_____ 1. hardy/stunted
_____ 2. sediment/silt
_____ 3. prolific/fertile
_____ 4. drought/deluge
_____ 5. nutrients/impurities
_____ 6. till/cultivate
_____ 7. thrive/prosper
_____ 8. residue/cream
_____ 9. heave/stomp

C. Use details from the selection to make a diagram of the soil cycle. Label each phase.

D. What is your dirt like? Scoop up a cupful and study it. Record as many observations as you can. Think like a pedologist!

E. Check your recall. Answer these factual questions on the back of this sheet.
   1. How did the early settlers of the prairie help to cause the Dust Bowl?
   2. How do plants make soil?
   3. How does water harm land?
   4. How do volcanoes grow pineapples?
   5. What is chernozem?

F. Choose a topic to research and write on:
   1. common soil conservation practices
   2. the Netherlands' practice of reclaiming soil from the sea
   3. dust bowl statistics
   4. sequoia trees

Name _____

Quite a Charge!

There is something electrifying about Roy C. Sullivan of Waynesboro, Virginia. He holds the dubious honor of having been hit by lightning more times than any other person on record—seven, to be exact. The strikes have occurred over a 30-year period and have left their mark on Mr. Sullivan's body. In 1942 lightning struck his big toe, knocking off the nail. Next strike, he lost his eyebrows, then his left shoulder was seared. His hair has been singed twice, and his legs and ankles injured. A hardy soul, Mr. Sullivan was on a fishing trip in 1977 when lightning paid its seventh visit, sending him to the hospital with stomach and chest burns. Mr. Sullivan is only one of more than 1,000 people who are hit by lightning in the United States every year. One hundred of those struck die, and many sustain much more serious injuries than Mr. Sullivan has experienced. Permanent brain damage and paralysis can occur in the half-second it takes for lightning to flash.

Lightning occurs when electrons in storm clouds are attracted to the positive charges built up in objects on the ground, especially at the tops of tall things like buildings, trees, poles, and towers. As many as 30 million volts of electricity can be generated when these positive and negative charges meet in the air. That is enough power to keep a 50-watt light bulb burning day and night for six months. Most people think lightning will never hit near them, but more than 8 million strikes occur each day worldwide. Lightning starts about 10,000 forest fires and burns homes and businesses worth more than $2 billion each year.

If you plan on outrunning lightning, think again. A jolt can travel over 60,000 miles per second. That is more than 1 billion miles an hour! Lightning can even run underground, erupting with a powerful charge many feet from where it first touched down. Most people think they are safe from lightning if it is not raining. The truth is that lightning can strike as far as ten miles away from an electrical storm. The one consolation for most of us is that more lightning strikes occur in rural areas than in populous ones.

A few precautions will keep most people from ever replicating Roy Sullivan's experiences with lightning. First, be a weather-watcher. Know when storms are predicted and stay alert. If lightning occurs while you are outside, postpone the ballgame and seek shelter in a building or a vehicle. If you must remain outdoors, stay away from tall objects such as flag poles and trees. Avoid mountaintops or open fields where your own body would be the tallest object present to draw the lightning. Squat down, put your hands over your ears to prevent hearing damage, and wait for the storm to pass.

Name _____

Quite a Charge!━━━━━━━━━━━━━━━━━▼

A. For each word write the letter of the correct definition.

_____ 1. dubious	a. pertaining to country life
_____ 2. sear	b. a comfort
_____ 3. singe	c. thickly inhabited
_____ 4. consolation	d. to brown a surface with heat
_____ 5. rural	e. doubtful
_____ 6. populous	f. to scorch
_____ 7. replicate	g. to duplicate

B. Answer these vocabulary questions on the back of this sheet.
1. Is there a difference between a *seared* steak and a *singed* one? Explain.
2. What famous children's story tells of the adventures of a *rural* rodent who visits his cousin in a *populous* place?
3. Give an example of a *dubious* honor you hold. Explain your feelings.
4. Why do contests award *consolation* prizes?
5. Would it be possible to *replicate* Mount Rushmore in your town? Explain.

C. For each paragraph in the reading selection, find the correct heading from the list below. Label I, II, III, and IV; you will have left-overs.
_____ 1. Where Lightning Strikes
_____ 2. First-Aid for Lightning-Struck Victims
_____ 3. One Lightning Victim and Statistics
_____ 4. How to Avoid Being Struck
_____ 5. History of Lightning
_____ 6. How Lightning Occurs and Statistics

D. Assume the identity of Roy C. Sullivan of Waynesboro, Virginia. Write a first-person account of your experience with lightning. How are you different because of the strikes?

E. For each statistic below, provide the correct number from the reading selection.
1. Number of people who die each year from lightning _____
2. Number who are struck each year by lightning _____
3. Number of seconds it takes for lightning to flash _____
4. Number of volts that can be generated _____
5. Number of forest fires started by lightning _____
6. Speed per second of lightning _____
7. Number of miles from a storm lightning can hit _____
8. Number of times Mr. Sullivan hit _____
9. Number of strikes per day around the world _____

Name _____

Surrealist Scene

It is a scene from real life but it stretches your imagination to the limits. Not even a surrealist could dream up a more fantastical place than the actual lake between Israel and Jordan known as the Dead Sea. To get to the lake, you descend steep, vividly colored cliffs to a rocky, barren plain. You are now standing at the lowest place on the surface of the earth, 1,320 feet below sea level. The white substance beneath your feet cracks and crunches as you walk past curious columns of salt rock. Then you notice the dead calm of the deep blue water. The sea is so dense, it does not even ripple in the breeze. The hot sun beats down unmercifully and you realize you have not seen one plant, one water creature, one bird.

The Dead Sea is the saltiest body of water in the world, about nine times as salty as any ocean. Thousands of gallons of river water flow into the lake each day, but none flows out. The water merely evaporates, leaving behind all the salts, silt, and chemicals from the river water. Though the environment is hostile to plant and animal life, workers collect the cracked crust along the lakeshore to extract minerals for table salt, fertilizers, and medicines. Some people believe that bathing in the briny lake is healthful, and tourists always enjoy floating in its buoyant waters.

A. Circle the best title.
   1. Harvest of Salt
   2. Curious Columns
   3. Deep and Salty
   4. Sea of Wild Dreams

B. On the back of this sheet, write an advertising slogan for each Dead Sea business listed here. Mention why the location is an advantage.
   1. Swimming classes for people afraid of sinking
   2. A nut and popcorn factory
   3. A golf course where you never lose balls hit in water
   4. A fishing resort for tired and lazy fishermen

C. For each word write the letter of the correct definition.
   _____ 1. surrealistic   a. thick with particles
   _____ 2. vivid   b. salty
   _____ 3. barren   c. an upright support
   _____ 4. column   d. marked by dream-like images
   _____ 5. dense   e. able to float
   _____ 6. unmercifully   f. bare, having few trees
   _____ 7. silt   g. mud brought by a river
   _____ 8. hostile   h. brilliant, intense
   _____ 9. briny   i. showing no forgiveness
   _____ 10. buoyant   j. showing ill will

A Losing Battle

The Great Western Erg can grow as tall as 600 feet, but it takes in no nourishment. It creeps forward at a pace of 36 feet a year and manages to do so without legs. It has been around since the Stone Age but alters its appearance daily. The Great Western Erg is the world's largest sand dune, covering about 15,000 square miles of the world's largest desert, the Sahara. Strong winds that blow across northern Africa sculpt the fine sand of the erg into a series of troughs and peaks that resemble ocean waves. Traveling the erg can be as treacherous as getting caught in a storm at sea. All throughout the year, seasonal winds bring their own unique perils. The Harmattan is a biting wind that blows in from the coast, covering everything in its path with choking red dust. The Khamsin blasts the erg for 50 endless days, and the dry, violent wind called the *Simoom* has been known to bury caravans, entire villages, even armies. Although the modern truck offers more desert protection than the camel caravan of old, the score in the Great Western remains unchanged to this day. In the battle with Sahara's wind and sand, man nearly always loses.

A. For each word write the letter of the correct definition.

_____ 1. nourishment   a. danger
_____ 2. alter   b. a company of travelers
_____ 3. trough   c. to change
_____ 4. peril   d. food
_____ 5. caravan   e. a low, narrow depression

B. Answer these vocabulary questions on the back of this sheet.
 1. Which would terrify you more, *peril* on an ocean, or peril at the Dead Sea? Explain.
 2. Many American colonists ate from *troughs*. Today, farm animals still do. Explain.
 3. What one detail of your life do you wish you could *alter*? Why?
 4. Think like a science fiction writer and imagine a way Martians get *nourishment*.
 5. Give three situations in which a car *caravan* might form.

C. Circle the best title.
 1. Ergs and Oases
 2. The Great Western Erg
 3. Winds of the World
 4. Desert Caravan
 5. The Sahara, Giant Sandbox

D. Look at a map. On the back of this sheet, list the 11 countries covered in part by the Sahara Desert.

E. We use directions to identify most North American winds. The people of the Sahara give each wind its own name. What conclusions could be drawn from this fact?

F. Write a folktale starring the three winds described in the selection. Use personification to give the winds personality traits.

Floating Flowers

His eyes dimmed with age, the old man struggled to scan the landscape. He was searching for one certain scene, a view so striking it would practically leap onto the canvas, despite his failing eyesight. Finally he found what he was looking for—in a pond near his country home. The last painting world-famous French impressionist Claude Monet ever made was of waterlilies. It was indeed his *magnum opus*, a masterpiece of color and sunlight captured in simple brushstrokes. With this painting, Monet caused the world to notice anew the incredible beauty and majesty of these colorful, floating flowers.

Horticulturalists agree with Monet—waterlilies are some of the most intriguing members of the plant world. More than 60 varieties grow in temperate and tropical environments, each floating in water as if it needed no soil to survive. In actuality, the waterlily grows from a tough rubbery stalk on the muddy bottoms of ponds, lakes, or slow-moving rivers. It reaches ten feet up to float large, flat leaves on the surface. In some locations, these leaves can grow five feet in diameter, strengthened by reinforcing ribs. Covered with a waxy coating, the leaves repel water and provide a surface useful for many purposes. Snails lay their eggs here, insects touch down for a moment's rest, frogs hide underneath, and, in the Amazon, the jacana, a bird with extremely long toes, uses the leaves for stepping stones as it searches the water's surface for food.

Most importantly, the unsinkable leaves provide the photosynthesis needed to produce the waterlily's colorful blossoms. When conditions are right, the plants spread easily, carried by water currents and breezes. Large numbers of blooms can clog rivers, but their roots trap pollutants and serve as excellent filters. Beds of waterlilies in bloom are a breathtaking sight; many visitors travel to Grass Lake, near Chicago, to view a stand that covers over 600 acres. Other enormous beds grow near New York City, in Monroe, Michigan, in southern California, Missouri, and Mississippi.

Every day, these flowers stage a water ballet, closing up tight during the night and early morning, opening at noon to display their colors, closing again at the first sign of wind or rain. This routine serves two functions: to open the flower for pollination when insects are most active, and to prolong its life. Unlike daisies or roses that bloom and fade in a few days' time, the waterlily blossom will live for weeks if left undisturbed.

Because of its incredibly long life, the flower was thought by ancient peoples to be immortal. Egyptians painted images of one type of waterlily, the lotus, on tombs and utensils intended to serve the dead in their afterlife. The Chinese regarded the flower as sacred, and India honors it to this day as one of its national symbols. Celebrated in worship and art, the waterlily blooms on as one of nature's most interesting plants.

Name _____

Floating Flowers ━━━━━━━━━━━━━━━━━━━━▼

A. For each quotation below, identify the correct speaker.
   1. "Dad, are we there yet? What's so great about a bunch of floating flowers, anyway?" _____
   2. "Open, close, open, close! That's all a poor girl does when the weather can't make up its mind." _____
   3. "Paint carefully, Tuta. Our mistress will want to be surrounded by the same beautiful flowers that she loved in this life." _____
   4. "Ah, there's a meal of bugs in that stump on the other side of the river. I'll cross on these handy pads." _____
   5. "Quickly! I must paint quickly! So much color and light to capture before my eyes give out." _____
   6. "It seems like I've grown for miles, and I still have not reached the surface." _____

B. Study a copy of Monet's famous waterlily painting. Create an acrostic poem for the word *water*, listing adjectives that apply.

   | W |
   | A |
   | T |
   | E |
   | R |

C. Research and write your findings on one of these topics:
   1. Claude Monet
   2. the South American jacana
   3. the lotus in ancient Egypt

D. Circle one of these titles and write your own short story.
   1. My *Magnum Opus*: A Painter's Last Strokes
   2. Life Among the Lilies: A Water Fantasy
   3. Stuck in the Mud: A Waterlily's Tall Tale

E. Write T for true or F for false.
   _____ 1. Waterlily leaves get soaked and decay quickly.
   _____ 2. Waterlilies do not grow in the ocean.
   _____ 3. Monet traveled days to view a famous bed of waterlilies.
   _____ 4. In the Amazon, birds build their nests on lily pads.
   _____ 5. Lilies close up only at night.
   _____ 6. Waterlilies grow all over the world, even blooming above the Arctic Circle.
   _____ 7. Lilies can be planted to help clean up dirty ponds and rivers.
   _____ 8. Too many waterlilies growing in a river can bring boating to a standstill.
   _____ 9. The lily's long root allows it to grow in deep, clear mountain lakes.
   _____ 10. The waterlily's waxy coating helps it float.

Desert Tall Tale

Some describe it as a prickly accordion plant, others use its Indian name, saguaro, but everyone agrees with the Latin designation for the world's largest cactus: *gigantea*. Found only in the deserts of southern Arizona, southeastern California, and northern Mexico, the saguaro cactus holds the world's record for height, growing as tall as 60 feet, the size of a five-story building. But this distinction is not attained overnight. It takes an average of ten years for the saguaro to grow one inch. Its first branch sprouts after 15 years. The plant blooms for the first time after 60 years—and then, only at night. Rain, or rather the lack of it, accounts for the infinitesimal growth rate. Showers in the desert, while rare, can be torrential, dumping several inches of water in a very short time. The saguaro traps every drop in ridges that run down its trunk. These ribs function much like an accordion, expanding after a rainfall, then shrinking as the plant slowly uses the water.

A. These sentences contain vocabulary words from the selection. Mark each C for correct or I for incorrect usage.

   _____ 1. At the town council meeting, the boys *attained* permission to rake leaves in the park for their scout project.

   _____ 2. The soccer coach gave him the *designation* of corner kicker.

   _____ 3. The *infinitesimal* size of the universe makes humans feel like ants.

   _____ 4. I have the *distinction* of being the only left-handed person in my family.

   _____ 5. The gentle patter of *torrential* rain on the roof soothed her to sleep.

B. Think and write.
   1. What distinction does the saguaro have? _____
   2. Does the saguaro have sharp spines? _____
   3. Is the saguaro as tall as the Empire State Building? _____
   4. When and how does the saguaro's diameter increase? _____

C. Draw your own conclusions. Discuss them with other members of your class.
   1. Moisture stored in big, soft petals evaporates quickly. How does this fact relate to the saguaro?
   2. Why has the state of Arizona made cactus rustling illegal?

D. Latin is the language of science. On the back of this sheet, list the Latin classifications for five of your favorite plants and animals. What do the Latin names mean?

E. Fact is often funnier than fiction. Create a humorous comic strip starring the saguaro cactus.

Northern Lights

Name _____

Tiny Eskimo children put fingers to their mouths and whistle into the darkening night. They are summoning the ghosts of green luminosity that often come to dance above their homes. Far off in the distance, the black sky begins to glow ominously. Arches and flickering bands of light come closer and closer. The children laugh nervously. A blaze of neon green suddenly appears right overhead and the children dash inside, almost believing that these specters in the sky will grab them and carry them off into the night.

Despite the children's faith in the old folk tale, the northern lights, or aurora borealis, will not harm them. Scientists now know that the spectacular light show is the result of a molecule collision high up in the atmosphere. The phenomenon begins when solar wind carries electrically charged particles from the sun close to the earth. Over the polar region, the particles bump into molecules in earth's atmosphere, releasing incredible light energy. No matter how science and legend differ, the aurora borealis will always be one of the world's most spectacular sights.

A. Give the topic sentence for this selection. _____

_____

B. These sentences contain vocabulary words from the selection. Mark each C for correct or I for incorrect usage.
    _____ 1. When the dog began to growl *ominously*, I backed off.
    _____ 2. Queen Isabel *summoned* Columbus to court so she could consider his grand plan once more.
    _____ 3. He worked as a *specter* for our company, checking the product for flaws before it was shipped out.
    _____ 4. El Niño is a weather *phenomenon* that brings unusual conditions to North and South America.
    _____ 5. The cave had an eery *luminosity*; we could not see even one pinprick of light.

C. Based on the selection, make a diagram on the back of this sheet, showing how the aurora borealis occurs. Label the steps.

D. The scientific name for the northern lights, aurora borealis, comes from mythology. Aurora, or dawn, was the sister of the Roman sun god. Boreas was the name of the Greek god of the north wind. Use a dictionary to find a mythological connection for each word here.
    1. martial arts_____ 2. insomnia _____
    3. cereal _____ 4. volcano _____
    5. hypnotism _____ 6. heliograph _____

Name _____

The Other Rain Forest

Rain falls daily, dripping from the dark green canopy of steamy, tangled vines and leaves to the darker layers below, where toucans caw, monkeys howl, and giant snakes slither. The scenery of the tropical rain forest is well-known to most people, but how many know of its equally fascinating twin, the temperate rain forest? Together, the rain forests of the Western Hemisphere, tropical and temperate, work in partnership to provide a home for more than 100 species of birds. It is time to pay attention to the temperate rain forest, to appreciate its contributions and to preserve its unique beauty.

Rain forests of the tropics are hot and humid year-round because of their location near the equator. The largest is the Amazon rain forest, located in South America. If you were to draw a line from this region going north, you would come to the Great Smoky Mountains in southeastern United States. Draw a second, longer line heading northwest, and you would eventually arrive in the Cascade Mountains of Oregon and Washington. Nestled in these mountain areas are the lush pockets that make up the temperate rain forests of the Western Hemisphere.

Like their warmer cousin, these temperate forests receive over 100 inches of precipitation a year. Odd as it seems for rain forests to get snow, temperatures here range from below zero in the winter to the high 90s in the summer. While trees in the tropics lose leaves and grow new ones all throughout the year, most of the trees of the temperate rain forest are deciduous. But like their southern partner, life occurs in layers, beginning with the sunny uppermost branches and filtering down to the cool, dark forest floor.

Over 2,300 species of vascular plants grow here, the most of any region in North America. Moisture-loving mosses, lichens, ferns, and fungi pop up from fallen logs and crevices. As these plants fall to the ground and decay, they become food for a host of small invertebrates: snails, slugs, and millipedes. Then, at night, millions of salamanders emerge to feed on the invertebrates. There are more kinds of salamanders here than anywhere else on earth.

Insects, invertebrates, and salamanders all become dinner for the migratory birds that raise their young in the temperate rain forests. When temperatures begin to drop, birds such as the yellow warbler, the oriole, and the wood thrush head south. They fly to spend the winter in the one place in the world most like their summer nesting grounds, the Amazon. In this way, the two rain forests work together to provide a stable environment for these species.

With so much attention going to tropical rain forests, we must not neglect our temperate ones, for they too are endangered. Logging and development, pollution and acid rain destroy acreage every day. Controlling these practices will help save both rain forests, tropical and temperate.

The Other Rain Forest

Name _____

A. For each word write the letter of the correct definition.

_____ 1. canopy   a. plants that absorb oxygen from the air
_____ 2. nestle   b. traveling from one home to another
_____ 3. lush   c. to lie close and snug
_____ 4. deciduous   d. a narrow crack
_____ 5. vascular   e. having leaves that fall off at certain seasons
_____ 6. lichens   f. dense growth
_____ 7. crevice   g. an overhanging shelter
_____ 8. invertebrates   h. having internal vessels for sap
_____ 9. emerge   i. animals lacking a backbone
_____ 10. migratory   j. to rise out of

B. For each sentence, supply the missing vocabulary word.
1. The hiker got his foot caught in a _____ on the mountain.
2. Plenty of irrigation keeps our lawn _____.
3. The _____ system distributes blood throughout the human body.
4. Nothing is more beautiful than early autumn in a _____ forest.
5. We held our breath as the tiny chick struggled to _____ from its shell.
6. My grandparents live a _____ lifestyle, spending the winter in Florida and the summer in Maine.
7. It is fun to _____ up with a blanket and a book on a cold, rainy afternoon.
8. Father pulled the car under the shop's canvas _____ so we could get in without getting soaked.
9. Many _____ animals form shells of amazing beauty and complexity
10. Scientists believe that rock-hugging _____ are among the world's oldest plants.

C. Label each characteristic below Temp, for the temperate rain forest, Trop for the tropical one, or B for both.
_____ 1. Located near the equator.
_____ 2. In danger of disappearing.
_____ 3. Experiences a wide variety of temperatures.
_____ 4. Receives snow.
_____ 5. Its trees lose leaves and grow new ones all year round.
_____ 6. Receives 100+ inches of precipitation a year.
_____ 7. Remains hot all year long.
_____ 8. Provides a summer home for migrant birds.
_____ 9. Life exists in different layers, from the tops of trees to the dark forest floor.
_____ 10. Is the home for more of the world's salamanders than anywhere else in the world.
_____ 11. Provides a winter home for migratory birds.
_____ 12. Its trees lose their leaves in the fall.

Name _____

Curious Carnivore

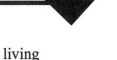

The dividing line between plant and animal kingdoms is clear-cut. Plants are the only living organisms in the world that engage in photosynthesis. No animal known to man can take its energy directly from the sun. On the animal side of the dividing line is rapid response to stimulation. All but two or three of the world's plants are incapable of swift movement. At the approach of an enemy or the sound of an alarm, an animal experiences an immediate reaction. Its heart speeds up, the eyes blink, the muscles tense, and the animal springs, howls, hops, or flies.

A few organisms, however, straddle the dividing line, taking characteristics from both plant and animal worlds. One of these, the Venus flytrap, is definitely a plant. It can live a healthy life entirely dependent on photosynthesis. But should an insect buzz too close to the flytrap's spreading leaves, the plant reacts as quickly as any animal, closing within 15 seconds around its unsuspecting prey. The secret to this quick response is the three long, stiff hairs located in the middle of each pair of leaves. The harder these hairs are hit, the more quickly the leaves will close. If by chance the plant traps some inedible object, the leaves will release it within a day or two. But if the object is a nice juicy insect, the leaves remain tightly shut, squeezing the prey against digestion glands. The plant then absorbs the dissolved parts of the insect. This process can take anywhere from 10 to 35 days, after which the leaves slowly open to reveal the dry shell remains of its meal. The wind clears the leftovers away, and the five-inch plant spreads itself innocently in the sun, waiting for the next unsuspecting victim to come too close. A regular diet of insects keeps the Venus flytrap glossy and vigorous.

Why does the flytrap thrive on meat? The answer is most likely found in examining the plant's natural habitat, a 60-mile area of bog in southeastern North Carolina. Here the wet, sandy soil lacks nitrogen, so the bugs captured by the flytrap's spiked leaves make up this deficiency. And at least once, the plant has been known to feed on something much larger than an insect. Shortly after World War II, *Life* magazine ran an amazing photograph taken by North Carolina naturalist and flytrap expert Will Rehder. Incredibly, Rehder's camera caught one of the bloodthirsty plants holding the lifeless body of a frog tightly between two leaves.

Name _____

Curious Carnivore ➤

A. For each word write the letter of the correct definition.
_____ 1. engage   a. a marsh
_____ 2. stimulation   b. activity designed to excite
_____ 3. straddle   c. to be busy with
_____ 4. vigorous   d. to favor two opposite sides
_____ 5. bog   e. a shortage
_____ 6. deficiency   f. full of strength and health

B. Write an original sentence for each word listed above, using the back of this sheet.

C. Research to find the answers.
1. One way scientists categorize living things is by their diets. List three creatures for each label: carnivore, herbivore, omnivore.
2. How is the Mimosa plant similar to the Venus flytrap? How is it different?

D. Write T for true or F for false.
_____ 1. The flytrap digests every particle of the insects it eats.
_____ 2. The flytrap eats only food containing nitrogen.
_____ 3. Within seconds the plant rejects objects it cannot eat.
_____ 4. The flytrap is healthiest when it is trapping and digesting insects.
_____ 5. Birds pick the hard remains of insects off the flytrap leaves.

E. On a sheet of plain white paper, make a chart that explains the difference between plants and animals. Show where the flytrap belongs.

F. What happens first? Number the quotations to show sequence.
_____ a. "Yum-yum, nitrogen at last!"
_____ b. "I'm open for business, but with this wind, I wonder how many meals will wander my way. . . "
_____ c. "Hey, the walls of this joint are closing in on me!"
_____ d. "Phooey, that's the third false alarm today. I'll just have to settle for a sip of sunshine."
_____ e. "I have to get out of this wind. Ah, those flat leaves down there will make a good landing strip."

G. Write three different captions that could go under the *Life* magazine photograph.

_____

_____

_____

The Tide That Towers ———————————————

Francisco de Orellana stared in amazement at the 15-foot wall of water racing toward the boat. His men pulled hard on their oars, but they were powerless to prevent the water from pushing them back up the Amazon River. The Spaniards did not know it but, on that exploratory trip of 1542, they were the first Europeans ever to witness the bore, a unique tide that takes place two times every day in a few places around the world.

A bore is created when an unusually high ocean tide rushes into the mouth of a river or bay. The banks forming the channel on either side are often high and narrow, which increases the force at which incoming water enters. The Amazon River crosses the entire width of the South American continent; it carries more water than any other river in the world. But, when it reaches the Atlantic, this mighty river is no match for the strong ocean currents off the coast of Brazil. They surge in, filling the channel in just a few seconds' time. Like normal tides all over the world, the bore is influenced by the moon. At certain times of year, the lunar phase almost completely empties the mouth of the Amazon. Then when the bore comes in, it is exceptionally high and powerful. Countless boats, large and small, have been caught off-guard and capsized during these times of peak tides. Bores occur in other places where ocean currents and land formations combine to create similar conditions. Besides the bore of the Amazon, the best-known are in Canada's Bay of Fundy and in the Qiantang River in China.

A. Listed below are the headings for an outline of the reading selection. Number them in order from 1 to 5.

   _____ 1. Amazon bore explained in detail
   _____ 2. Other examples given
   _____ 3. Definition of a bore
   _____ 4. First sighting of Amazon bore
   _____ 5. Possible dangers of a bore

B. English is a puzzling language. Many of its words can have several entirely different meanings. *Bore* can be a noun that refers to a tide, or either of two verbs, to drill a hole or to weary with dullness. Change the spelling to *boar* and you have a homophone, a word that sounds the same, but with a different spelling and a different meaning.

  1. Give at least two meanings for each of these words:
     bear, rest, bark, blow, purse, till, wind _____

     _____

     _____

  2. List homophones for each of these words: *birth, grown, aloud, peel, course, berry, miner, seller, flower, choose, cereal, kernel, sight, bare, fair* _____

     _____

C. Research to learn more about Francisco de Orellana's fascinating journey down the Amazon River.

Sand Trap

Name _____

It is the largest sand hill anywhere on the eastern coast of the United States, standing over 130 feet high. Jockey's Ridge on the Outer Banks of North Carolina got its name because its steep sides form a natural racetrack complete with seating. Ever since the first horses escaped from Spanish explorers and formed wild herds near the dunes, people have raced here. Jockeys spur their animals down the bank to cheers of spectators seated on the sandy rim. But a dangerous obstacle awaits riders at the foot of the ridge—quicksand.

On the western side of the dune, the sand is so fine that rain does not drain through. The grains in this deep pocket remain suspended in water long after other dunes have dried. The sand moves like water, almost as if it were alive, which is actually the old meaning of the word *quick*. A thick crust forms on top which appears to be solid, but it cannot support objects heavier than twigs or dried leaves. Over the years, many horses and even several cars have been swallowed by this pit of sand. How far down their remains have settled, no one knows. If you get caught in quicksand at Jockey's Ridge or anywhere else, stay calm. Assume the back-float position, with arms and legs outstretched. Because quicksand is essentially water, your body will slowly float to the top. Then carefully roll to solid ground. Quicksand is deadly only to those who do not know what to do.

A. Write T for true or F for false.

_____ 1. The wild horses of today's Outer Banks descended from those brought by Spanish explorers.

_____ 2. The quicksand of Jockey's Ridge sometimes dries up.

_____ 3. The sand is called *quick* because of its swift movement.

_____ 4. Quicksand behaves more like sand than water.

_____ 5. If you get caught in quicksand, grab for the crust.

B. Our language is constantly changing. New words are created and old ones pick up different shades of meaning. The word *quick* is one example of a word whose meaning has changed over the years. For each of the words below, use a dictionary to discover the original meaning. How has that meaning changed over the years?

1. silly _____   4. pretty _____

2. husband _____   5. minister _____

3. stout_____   6. happy _____

C. The Outer Banks has been the scene of several interesting events. Choose a topic below to research.

1. Roanoke, the lost colony

2. the Wright brothers

3. Blackbeard and the age of piracy

Recess for Rocks

"Class dismissed!" Those are beautiful words to almost any student. But none have been more excited about recess than the sixth graders in the farming community of Parral, Mexico, in the winter of 1969.

Sky-watchers reported that a meteorite shower had peppered the foothills of Parral with unusual rocks from outer space. Experts from the Smithsonian's Museum of Natural History in Washington, D.C., rushed to Parral and convinced school officials to release the students to help search for the meteorites. Thirty-six boys fanned out across the fields. Within minutes, they spotted the first black-and-white rock. The scientists were stunned. A few other meteorites of this type had been found before, but none of this size. Over the course of the day, the boys of Parral found many samples, ranging from 4 to 20 pounds. For the first time ever, experts would have enough material for in-depth analysis.

Rocks were shipped to labs all over the world and the tedious work of the cosmochemists began. They learned that the white streaks in the meteorites were much older than the black rock that surrounded them. The CAIs, or calciumaluminum inclusions, most likely came from the explosion of an enormous star during the formation of the solar system.

A few months later, NASA brought home the first rocks gathered from the surface of the moon. Excitement in the scientific community was high. What new information would this lunar material yield? Compared with the meteorites from Parral, these rocks were disappointing. Who would have ever guessed that a school recess would yield more about the origins of the universe than a mission to the moon?

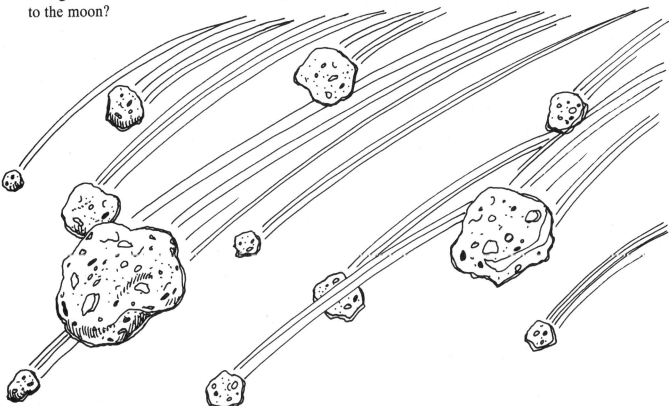

Recess for Rocks

Name _____

A. Circle the best headline for a newspaper article on this topic.
   1. Meteorites Found in Mexican Foothills
   2. Smithsonian Studies Mysterious Stones
   3. NASA Disappointed in Moon Rock Findings
   4. Kids' Rock Hunt Reveals Age of Universe
   5. Budding Cosmochemists Go on Recess

B. Put yourself in the Parral boys' shoes. What thoughts cross your mind as you hold the oldest known thing in the universe in your hand? Share your thoughts with the class.

C. What happened first? Number the statements in chronological order from 1 to 5.

   _____ 1. Scientists analyze the Mexican meteorites.

   _____ 2. Smithsonian officials hear news of the meteorite shower.

   _____ 3. Apollo XI brings home lunar rocks.

   _____ 4. Parral students assist in the search for rocks.

   _____ 5. A meteorite shower scatters rocks throughout the countryside of Parral, Mexico.

D. A good scientist needs to be a good writer in order to explain his/her discoveries to the world. Find an actual rock that interests you. Study that rock closely and write an accurate description of its features on notebook paper.

E. Design a brochure complete with pictures and captions that will attract tourists to the area in which the meteorites were found.

F. Write T for true or F for false.

   _____ 1. The analysis of the Parral rocks was performed in Washington, D. C.

   _____ 2. Cosmochemistry is the study of matter originating beyond the earth's atmosphere.

   _____ 3. The meteorite hunt was for male students only.

   _____ 4. The Parral meteorites were the first of that kind of rock ever to be found.

   _____ 5. NASA scientists knew ahead of time that the Parral rocks were older than anything they would find on the moon.

Answer Key

ANCIENT DAZE

The U.S. Camel Corps

A. 1. g, 2. c, 3. e, 4. h, 5. d, 6. a, 7. f, 8. b

B. 1. Tooth Fairy, Porky Pig, Paul Bunyan
   2. You could give yourself an exotic look by coloring and cutting your hair and by wearing foreign clothes.
   3. Answers will vary.
   4. Answers will vary.
   5. Teenagers enjoy ridiculing one another for fun and do it frequently.
   6. Answers will vary.

C. Answers will vary. Suggestions follow:
   1. "I hope, gentlemen, you will suspend your disbelief long enough to hear my defense of these noble beasts."
   2. "Millie, quick! Run get the children! The circus has made it all the way to Texas!"
   3. "It's all over. I'm a goner. The heat has finally fried my brain. I just thought I saw a tall, hairy monster go behind that hill."

D. 1. T, 2. F, 3. F, 4. F, 5. T, 6. F, 7. T, 8. F

Peacock Pilgrims

page 4

A. The Pilgrims loved to wear bright colors.

B. 1. blue, 2. green, 3. brown, 4. green, 5. brown, 6. red, 7. brown, 8. red, 9. purple, 10. blue, 11. yellow, 12. red

C. 1. prolong
   2. diverse
   3. testimony
   4. somber
   5. leisure
   6. prosperity
   7. notion
   8. attired/clad
   9. occupation
   10. clad/attired
   11. garment
   12. maroon

D. Answers will vary.

E. Answers will vary.

Father of Gadgets

page 5

A. Answers will vary.

B. Answers will vary.

C. John Montagu, fourth Earl of Sandwich, is credited with creating the meal eaten between two pieces of bread, which allowed him to eat and gamble on card games at the same time. *Mesmerize* came from the name of a famous Austrian who hypnotized patients. Maverick was the last name of a Texas cattle rancher who refused to brand his calves as other ranchers did. Mrs. Amelia Bloomer was the first prominent woman to wear the loose style of women's short trousers in public. J. R. Poinsett of South Carolina brought the first "Christmas" flowers to the United States. Monsieur Leotard was a French high-wire artist who performed in a short, tight, sleeveless garment. Sylvester Graham was an American doctor who advocated a diet of flour made from entire wheat kernels. A. E. Burnside, a general in the Union Army, became known for his bushy side whiskers.

D. *genius, degenerate, indigenous, ingenue, regenerate, gene, genuine, disingenuous, genetics, gender, generous, progeny, gentry, gentleman, genteel, genre, genial, gentile*

SOS

page 6

A. Answers will vary.

B. What: .-- ... .- -
   God: --. --- -..
   Hath: .... .- - ....
   Wrought: .-- .-. --- ..- --. .... -

C. 1. United Nations International Children's Emergency Fund
   2. absent without leave
   3. very important person
   4. radio detecting and ranging
   5. Répondez, S'il Vous Plâit
   6. Organization of Petroleum Exporting Countries
   7. sound navigating and ranging
   8. National Aeronautics and Space Administration
   9. North Atlantic Treaty Organization
   10. Zoning Improvement Plan

D. Samuel Morse was passionate about art as a young man. He became known for his portraits and historical paintings but did not earn enough money to be financially secure during the 20 years he painted. His work with the telegraph was begun in an attempt to secure the independence that would allow Morse to paint as he pleased. The project consumed so much of his mind and time, however, that Morse never returned to painting. He spent the last 30 years of his life developing the telegraph industry and became involved in politics.

E. Answers will vary.

For Vanity's Sake

page 8

A. 1. h, 2. f, 3. d, 4. j, 5. i, 6. c, 7. e, 8. a, 9. g, 10. b

B. Answers will vary.

C. Since the dawn of time, people have used cosmetics to enhance their appearance.

D. 2

E. 1. beetle eye glitter
   2. blue beards
   3. orange-dyed hands

F. 1. a Roman soldier
   2. an Egyptian lover
   3. a Saxon warrior

G. Answers will vary.

H. 1. Kabuki theater features stock characters in exaggerated melodramas. The characters are easily identified by their colorful, dramatic makeup.
   2. Native Americans traditionally used face paint to protect their skin from sun and cold, to indicate achievement of adulthood, to inspire each other to valor in battle, and in ceremonial dances.

Peking to Paris Proof page 10

A. 1. 40, 2. 2, 3. 6, 4. 10,000, 5. 61, 6. 8, 7. 1901, 8. 5, 9. 81, 10. 3, 11. 14, 12. 4

B. Answers will vary. Suggestions follow:
1. The race probably helped sell more papers because people wanted to read of the drivers' progress and adventures. When three contestants successfully completed the race, the paper gained credibility.
2. The successful completion of the race helped convince average citizens that the car was a dependable means of transportation. If it could stand up to the challenges of mountain and desert, it could handle more civilized roads.

C. 1. 9, 2. 8, 3. 2, 4. 7, 5. 10, 6. 6, 7. 1, 8. 4, 9. 5, 10. 3

D. Answers will vary.

Pole Position page 11

A. 1. b, 2. c, 3. d, 4. e, 5. a

B. 1. Answers will vary.
2. Answers will vary.
3. If light shows through the paper or cloth, it is translucent.
4. Answers will vary.

C. 1. Student diagrams should show: an underground dugout, whalebones, roof of straw and dirt, membranes across windows, smokehole, and pole.
2. A fire station pole is usually made from polished wood or metal. Its sole purpose is to allow quick descent. The barabara pole was made from a rough tree trunk. Because it was used for going up and down, it might have had notches along its surface.
3. Advantages: warm and cozy in winter, providing protection from animals and enemies.
Disadvantages: little light, tight quarters, possibilities of leaking roof or cave-in, possibly smoky.

D. Answers will vary.

E. The tipi was a cone-shaped tent used by the Plains Indians. Made of hides and poles, it was easy to take down as the tribe followed the herds of buffalo. The iglu was a temporary Eskimo hunting lodge made of blocks of ice, with snow packed in the cracks and lined with fur. The pueblo was a multi-storied, apartment-style town built by Southwestern tribes from adobe. The longhouse was a log cabin-style, permanent dwelling built by the Eastern Woodland tribes. It provided shelter for several families. A wickiup was a Native-American hut made of brush wood or covered with mats.

Sweet Kiss page 12

A. 1. T 2. F 3. F 4. F 5. F

B. Answers will vary.

C. 1. as seen from above
2. to move slowly
3. eye wrinkles
4. an easy life
5. very scarce
6. a scoundrel in disguise
Sentences will vary.

D. The small size of the Kiss fools people into thinking they are not eating very much fattening candy. People also like the convenience of the one-bite size—no messy fingers from melting chocolate. Other foods being produced in bite size: Bagel Bites, ice cream sandwiches, peanut-butter crackers, taco chips.

The Travels of Plants page 14

A. 5

B. When man steps in to aid these natural travel plans, the results are often mixed. This selection concludes that we should continue planting growing things where we need them, but only after careful thought about the environmental effects.

C. 1. F, 2. F, 3. T, 4. F, 5. F, 6. T, 7. F, 8. T, 9. T, 10. F

D. Answers will vary.

E. 1. h, 2. d, 3. g, 4. b, 5. e, 6. a, 7. a, 8. f, 9. i, 10. c

The Mysterious Smile page 16

A. 1. c, 2. g, 3. e, 4. h, 5. a, 6. b, 7. i, 8. j, 9. f, 10. d

B. 1. Disputes
2. sumptuous
3. theory
4. Shrouded
5. compensation
6. plagued
7. perceive
8. relinquish
9. resolve
10. identity

C. What is Mona Lisa looking at?
What is the reason for her sad smile?
Why does she wear dark clothes?
Why did the painting take so long?
Why was the painting never delivered?
Why did Leonardo take the painting to France?
Students' solutions to questions will vary.

D. Answers will vary.

Pie in the Sky page 17

A. 1. d, 2. f, 3. a, 4. e, 5. c, 6. b

B. Answers will vary.

C. Answers will vary.

D. Answers will vary.

E. The yo-yo was a weapon used in the Philippines to ensnare an animal by the legs. Donald Duncan saw it in the 1920s and scaled it down in size to become a toy. The hula hoop was used by children in ancient Egypt and Greece. The first hoops were made from dried grapevines. English children in the nineteenth century twirled wooden and metal hoops around their waists. Marbles began as the knucklebones of sacrificial animals, used by priests to prophesy. Later, they were made from polished stones and clay. The kite first appeared in China in 1200 B.C. as a military signalling device.

Hero's Army   **page 18**
  A. Diagram should show: coin, slot, and lever action
      releasing an item.
  B. In A.D. 60, Hero mounted a small, hollow globe
      on a pipe which ran to a steam kettle. There were
      two L-shaped pipes fastened on either side of the
      globe. When the steam rushed into the globe, it
      began to spin—the first steam engine. It did not,
      however, perform any useful work. The screw
      press extracted juice from grapes and olives. It
      consisted of a threaded shaft attached to a wooden
      block. This device enabled the user to apply
      greater pressure than earlier presses had.
  C. Answers will vary.
  D. Answers will vary.
  E. Answers will vary.

The Lost State of Franklin   **page 20**
  A. 1. 2, 2. 4, 3. 5, 4. 3, 5. 1
  B. 1. Benjamin Franklin
      2. North Carolina government officials
      3. John Sevier's wife
      4. John Sevier
  C. Answers will vary.
  D. Answers will vary.
  E. 1. C, 2. C, 3. I, 4. I, 5. C, 6. C
  F. According to the Bible, the Garden of Eden was
      the perfect home God designed for Adam and Eve.
      They could have lived there forever if they had not
      sinned against God. Shangri-La is the name James
      Hilton created for an ideal Tibetan mountain
      village in his 1933 novel, *Lost Horizon*. Atlantis
      was a perfect island that the ancient Greeks
      believed sank into the ocean during an earthquake.
      Utopia was another fictitious island where laws
      and politics were perfect. It was the title of a 1516
      book by Sir Thomas More.

Tulipomania   **page 22**
  A. 1. C, 2. C, 3. C, 4. I, 5. C, 6. I, 7. C, 8. I, 9. I, 10. I
  B. 1500–tulips grow in Turkey
      1550–first tulips sent to Europe
      1555–tulips grow in gardens of wealthy +
      1593–tulips grow in common gardens -
      1632–multicolored tulips appear +
      1637–government regulates prices -
      1645–bulb sales begin to increase around the world +
  C. Answers will vary.
  D. Answers will vary.
  E. Annuals: morning glories, asters, zinnias,
      marigolds, snapdragons Perennials: daffodils, iris,
      monarda, tulips, lilies
  F. Answers will vary.
  G. 1. fascination with fire
      2. fascination with stealing
      3. fascination with England
      4. fascination with the Beatles
      5. fear of water
      6. fear of closed spaces
      7. fear of open spaces
      8. fear of light

Brick by Brick   **page 24**
  A. 1. F, 2. T, 3. F, 4. F, 5. F, 6. T, 7. F, 8. T, 9. F, 10. T
  B. Answers will vary.
  C. Answers will vary. The greatest number of
      combinations possible in #3 is 24.
  D. Answers will vary.
  E. Similarities: both were poor men from Denmark,
      they shared a name in common, they both gave
      children a wonderful gift. Differences: Ole married
      and had children, Hans remained single. Ole
      worked with his hands to make his own way, Hans
      had patrons throughout his life.

Code-Talkers   **page 25**
  A. 1. The Navaho land was so poor for farming or
         ranching, no one else wanted it.
      2. Under the land were rich coal deposits which
         today earn millions for the tribe.
      3. Diné, the People
      4. They are used in ceremonies, most often for
         healing.
  B. 1. e, 2. c, 3. f, 4. h, 5. i, 6. d, 7. a, 8. g, 9. b
  C. 1. e, 2. d, 3. f, 4. a, 5. b, 6. c

If the Shoe Fits   **page 26**
  A. 1. b, 2. d, 3. f, 4. c, 5. a, 6. e
  B. 1. weddings and funerals
      2. Answers will vary.
      3. Give candy and compliments, flirt, be yourself,
         dress attractively.
      4. Answers will vary.
      5. During rainy ones
      6. Thumbtacks, pins, staples, tape
  C. Answers will vary.
  D. Answers will vary

Chuckwagon Wonder   **page 28**
  A. Check: 1, 5, 7, 8, 10; Plus: 2, 3, 4, 6, 9
  B. 2. Being a trail cook often brought out the best in
         a man.
      3. Some crews treated their cooks with courtesy.
      4. To some men, the quantity of food was more
         important than the quality.
      6. "Grub-Wrangler" was sometimes used as a term
         of respect.
      9. Most cowboys appreciated a little entertainment
         to liven up the lonely nights.
  C. Similarities: both men work with food, often
      creating something delicious from ordinary or
      limited ingredients; they both have to please a
      variety of people; both jobs are sometimes
      physically hard. Differences: The modern-day chef
      is celebrated in the media while the trail cook was
      known only to his men. The chef often makes very
      good money and can open several restaurants. The
      trail cook might have made good pay but only
      worked during trail drives. The chef has the latest
      in spotless, sophisticated equipment, while the
      cook used only two or three utensils.
  D. 1. f, 2. c, 3. h, 4. j, 5. d, 6. a, 7. i, 8. g, 9. e, 10. b
  E. Answers will vary.
  F. Answers will vary.

PEOPLE TO PONDER

A Different Life   page 30
A. Actual answers will vary. "I taste an alcoholic beverage never fermented, from cups made of oyster shell."
B. 1. T, 2. F, 3. F, 4. T, 5. F, 6. F, 7. T, 8. T, 9. F, 10. F, 11. F, 12. T
C., D., E., F. Answers will vary.

A Voice for the Seas   page 31
A. Answers will vary.
B. Oil spills are the primary cause of ocean pollution, from tankers, pipelines, and cracks in the ocean floor. Sixteen billion pounds of plastic are dumped annually into the world's oceans, proving especially harmful to wildlife. Scientists believe pollution causes red tide, a sudden bloom of microscopic animals due to raised temperatures and chemical levels of the water. Offshore drilling for oil accounts for 20% of the world's supply. It is the most dangerous and costly method of extracting oil. The UN regulates ocean ownership, policing treaties that limit fishing rights and protect the environment. It also seeks to protect certain species of fish which are in danger of extinction due to over-fishing.
C. Answers will vary.

24 Hours of Power   page 32
A. 3
B. Answers will vary.
C. 1. 4, 2. 2, 3. 8, 4. 1, 5. 3, 6. 6, 7. 7, 8. 5

Baby Island Baby Sitter   page 34
A. 1. d, 2. b, 3. e, 4. a, 5. c
B. 1. cut, color, curl hair 2. , 3. , 4. Answers will vary.
   5. Tom Thumb, Thumbelina, Tinkerbelle, the Lilliputians
C. S=smoke, steam, U=under the sea, R=rumbling, T=terrific pressure, S=shaking, splitting, E=eruption, Y=youngest place on earth
D. 1. The apple core would add nutrients to the soil; the seed could grow and produce fruit.
   2. likes being alone, interested in nature, brave, sharp observer, forceful with unwelcome visitors
   3. Because fire from the earth caused the island to be born, it is fitting to name it after the fire god.
   4. Answers will vary.
E. 1. 6, 2. 3, 3. 8, 4. 2, 5. 4, 6. 1, 7. 7, 8. 5

King of "Mosts"   page 35
A. 1. f, 2. d, 3. i, 4. e, 5. h, 6. a, 7. g, 8. c, 9. b
B. Answers will vary.
C. 1, 2, 3: Answers will vary.
D. astrology—stars, audiology—hearing, cardiology—heart, seismology—earthquakes, dermatology—skin, ichthyology—fish

Dr. Seuss on the Loose   page 36
A. Answers will vary.
B. 1. b, c, 2. a, 3. c, 4. c, d, 5. a, b, 6. b

C. If Dr. Seuss had given up searching for a publisher, he probably never would have written more books for children. Children who could not find interesting books to read would not have developed into good readers.

Final Flight   page 38
A. 1. f, 2. c, 3. a, 4. b, 5. e, 6. d
B. 1. famous African-American educator
   2. champion of women's voting rights
   3. first woman elected governor, Wyoming, 1925
   4. introduced cash crop of indigo to South Carolina planters
   5. first important African-American tennis player
   6. one of the greatest stage actresses of all time
C. 2
D. 1, 2, Answers will vary.
E. 1. 4, 2. 6, 3. 2, 4. 5, 5. 1, 6. 3
F. Answers will vary.

The Collector-Collector   page 40
A. Collector: keen eyes, eager to learn, willing to travel; collector-collector: good motivator, encourager, able to anticipate collectors' needs; Baird knew how to help collectors because he himself had been one.
B. A museum preserves and celebrates the past, it explains why things exist in the present form, and in its variety it offers suggestions to try in the future.
C. Answers will vary.
D. 1. Baird's mother or father
   2. a museum visitor
   3. a collector in a remote place
   4. Baird
E. 1. Peter Pan
   2. Cinderella
   3. Humpty Dumpty
   4. Pinocchio
   5. Gulliver
   6. Noah
   7. Sleeping Beauty

A Foot in Two Worlds   page 41
A. Pocahontas stood as a living link between two drastically different cultures, and, at her death, they split angrily apart, not reconciling until many years and lives had been tragically wasted.
B. Answers will vary.
C. 1. Wichita, Iowa, Missouri, Omaha, Dakota, Winnebago, Seattle, Yakima, Spokane, Pasquotank, Yamasee, Yazoo, Biloxi, Catawba, Natchez, Yuma, Peoria, Ottawa, Massachusetts, Miami, Huron, Oneida, Susquehanna, Caribbean, Minnesota, Mississippi, Manitoba, Saskatchewan, Utah, Nebraska.
   2. Use a chamois to polish the car. Mother fixed succotash for supper. Quinine relieves the symptoms of malaria. Chinquapins are good shade trees. Large herds of caribou roam in Greenland. Tatoos once had religious significance. They carried their belongings on a travois. Jerky makes a good trail snack. Guava jelly is delicious on toast! Wool from the alpaca is soft and fine. Cattle graze on the pampas of Argentina.

D. 1. a chief from another branch of the Powhatan tribe
   2. the English
   3. Rebecca
   4. they called her "Princess"

Comic Book Code Breaker   page 42
A. 1. F, 2. T, 3. F, 4. F, 5. F
B. Without the preconceived notions adults have learned, children can often see quickly and clearly into the heart of a problem.
C., D. Answers will vary.

Mary's Madness   page 44
A. Answers will vary.
B. Keen eyes, strong back, patience, intelligence, curiosity, delicate touch, persistence, love of outdoors, imagination, intuition
C. Great Britain had just joined with Ireland to become the United Kingdom, the first steam railroads beginning; in France Napoleon was building his empire; the U.S. was on the brink of war with England over shipping rights, had just outlawed the importing of slaves from Africa; China was experiencing a population explosion and rebellion; Japan was closed to the outside world; Islam was spreading through western Africa, while the Zulus controlled the south.
D. 1. other lizard
   2. arm lizard
   3. double beam
   4. bent lizard
   5. cover lizard
   6. rough tooth
   7. curved lizard
   8. first horn face
   9. three horn face
   10. iguana tooth lizard
   11. king of tyrant lizards
   12. near lizard
   13. toothless wing
   14. ancient feather
E. 1. T, 2. F, 3. F, 4. T, 5. T, 6. F, 7. F, 8. T

The Will to Run   page 46
A. 1. trying for college scholarship
   2. at birth
   3. when tonsils removed
   4. when brace put on leg
   5. at four years old
B. Answers will vary.
C. Jesse Owen was an African-American Olympic runner, Jim Thorpe was a Native-American track star, Babe Zaharias was a great female golfer, Johnny Weismuller was an Olympic swimmer and "Tarzan" star, Sonja Henie was an Olympic ice skater and movie star, Esther Williams was an Olympic swimmer and movie star.
D. 1. d, 2. f, 3. b, 4. e, 5. a, 6. g, 7. h, 8. j, 9. c, 10. i

Polar Friendship   page 48
A. 1. c, 2. f, 3. i, 4. g, 5. b, 6. d, 7. h, 8. a, 9. j, 10. e
B. Answers will vary.

C. 1. H, 2. P, 3. P, 4. H, 5. P, 6. H, 7. H, 8. P
D. Richard E. Byrd and Floyd Bennett were the first to reach the North Pole by airplane; Sir John Franklin led an Arctic expedition in 1845 that vanished; William Baffin searched for the Northwest Passage in 1615 and 1616; the USS *Nautilus* was the first submarine to pass under the Pole; in 1978 Naomi Uemura made a solo trip by dog sled; Roald Amundsen made the first complete Northwest Passage by boat in 1906; Henry Hudson explored the Arctic regions until he disappeared in 1611.
E. Answers will vary.

War Host   page 49
A. 3
B. Answers will vary.

Vegetable Inventor   page 50
A. Answers will vary.
B. Answers will vary.
C. 1. smoke+fog
   2. motor+hotel
   3. breakfast+lunch
   4. scamper+ hurry
   5. squeeze+crunch
   6. chuckle+snort
D. Answers will vary.

The Cannonball Sisters   page 51
A. 1. c, 2. e, 3. a, 4. d, 5. b
B. Answers will vary.
C. 1. Sally Ride was the first American female to travel in space; Marie Curie was a Polish chemist who discovered radioactivity; Anne Boney was a female pirate; Nellie Bly was an investigative reporter; Sojourner Truth was an Underground Railroad operator; Annie Oakley was a sharpshooter with Buffalo Bill's Wild West Show
   2. Answers will vary.

The Power of Observation   page 52
A. Quality inspector, restorer of antiques and paintings, air traffic controller, trail guide, security guard.
B., C., D. Answers will vary.

MASTER DISASTERS
All for the Love of Sugar   page 54
A. 1. c, 2. d, 3. f, 4. h, 5. g, 6. a, 7. e, 8. b
B. 1. derivative   5. cargo
   2. eclipsed   6. enterprising
   3. indigenous   7. boll
   4. legacy   8. Crusaders
C. 1. large numbers of Crusaders would not have traveled there
   2. farmers would never have tried African slaves
   3. slavery should have died out sooner in the U.S.
   4. we would not have to fight prejudice and discrimination
   5. we would have a land of more opportunity
D. 1. a separation of the races, a glorification of the plantation lifestyle, resentment, bigotry, prejudice, fear, stereotyping

2. endurance, strength, control of emotions, rich imagination, ability to survive great odds, skill or trade

Death in the Clouds   page 55
A. After safe record transporting bombers and passengers, dirigible *Hindenburg* exploded, ending air-ship era.
B. Answers will vary.
C. The more people travel, the more accidents occur, and the less horrible they seem.

Quake!   page 56
A. 1. F, 2. F, 3. F, 4. T, 5. F
B. Answers will vary.
C. Jack London: 1876-1916, participated in the Klondike Gold Rush, wrote *The Call of the Wild* and other adventure books. Enrico Caruso: 1873-1921, an Italian tenor, one of the greatest opera stars of his day. John Barrymore: 1882-1942, an outstanding stage and movie actor, battled alcoholism.

Viral Killer   page 58
A. 1. a parent during second polio outbreak
   2. Mrs. Salk
   3. a child observing Franklin Roosevelt
   4. a parent today
   5. a doctor seeing the start of the second outbreak
B. Answers will vary.
C. 1. The son of a garment worker, he worked after school and earned scholarships.
   2. He refused to accept them.
   3. He worked on developing flu shots.
D. 1. 1950   6. 1915
   2. 1915   7. 1950
   3. 1950   8. 1950
   4. 1950   9. 1915
   5. 1950   10. 1950
E. Answers will vary.

The Johnstown Flood   page 59
A. 1. overwhelm
   2. trash
   3. lessen
   4. greatness
   5. assemble
B. 1. d, 2. e, 3. a, 4. c, 5. b
C. Answers will vary.

Ordeal by Hunger   page 60
A. 1. F, 2. T, 3. F, 4. F, 5. T, 6. F, 7. T, 8. T
B. Differences: some animals eat other animals, even their own babies, some do not raise their children, they do not decorate their environments, they do not wear clothes.
   Similarities: both need food, air, water, shelter. Most respond to love and care.
C. Answers will vary.

Island Mystery   page 61
A. Answers will vary.
B. 1. 5   2. 2   3. 7   4. 4   5. 1   6. 6   7. 3
C. Answers will vary.

Unlucky Ladies   page 62
All answers will vary.

Blood Ties   page 64
A. 1. M   2. T, M, A   3. T, A   4. T   5. M, A   6. A
   7. T, M, A   8. T, M   9. M   10. A   11. M   12. T
   13. A
B. Answers will vary.
C. Answers will vary.
D. Jim Bowie: 1796-1836, famous frontiersman, developed dangerous hunting knife, born in Kentucky, moved to Texas as a young man, led in early struggles against Mexico. Davy Crockett: 1786-1836, famous hunter, scout, soldier, Congressman, teller of yarns, born in Tennessee, moved to Texas later in life. Sparta's soldiers: best-trained soldiers of the ancient world, began at age 7, did not learn to read or write, but lived harshly to prepare for hardships of battle. Xerxes I: ruled Persia, spent years trying to conquer all of Greece, burned down Athens, finally killed by his own men who were tired of battle. Eleazer Ben Jair and the Sicarii: Jewish patriots who fought an armed rebellion against Roman rule, captured Masada in A.D. 66, held for six years before they burned their own camp and killed their families rather than surrender.
E. Answers will vary.

Telescope Through Time   page 66
A. 1. e, 2. f, 3. c, 4. h, 5. a, 6. d, 7. g, 8. b
B. 1. e, 2. f, 3. g, 4. a, 5. d, 6. b, 7. c
C. 3
D. 1. Mexico, 1982
   2. Philippines, 1951
   3. Mexico, 1943
   4. Indonesia, 1883
   5. Alaska, 1912
   6. Ecuador, 1877
   7. Washington, 1980
   8. Sicily, 1669
   9. Martinique, 1902
E. Answers will vary.

Drastic Drama   page 68
A. 1. c, 2. f, 3. h, 4. g, 5. b, 6. d, 7. a, 8. e
B. 1. derringer   5. yearn
   2. usurp   6. optimistic
   3. implement   7. crazed
   4. cowering   8. Adrenaline
C. 3
D. 1. B, 2. L, B, 3. L, 4. L, J, 5. B, 6. J, 7. L, B, 8. L, J

The Day the Dollar Died   **page 70**
A. 1. O, 2. O, 3. F, 4. O, 5. F, 6. O, 7. F, 8. O, 9. F, 10. O
B., C. Answers will vary.
D. 1. d, 2. f, 3. b, 4. i, 5. a, 6. g, 7. e, 8. h, 9. c

The Trail of Tears   **page 71**
A. Any one will work; look for student's reasoning.
B. so we do not let the same problems reoccur, so we remember and honor those who suffered, so we can teach future generations
C. Differences: white settlers were not forced to go, usually were well-provisioned. Similarities: faced the same dangers on the trail
D. John Ross: 1790-1866, Cherokee chief, fought U.S. government's removal policy in court, led people on trail West; Stand Watie: only Indian general in the Confederate army, one of last to surrender in the Civil War; Maria Tallchief: born 1925, part Osage Indian, first American-trained ballerina of international importance; Sequoyah: 1760-1843, Cherokee, invented system of writing for his language, helped settle disputes with U.S. government in move West; Will Rogers: 1879-1935, part Cherokee, cowboy humorist, author, radio and vaudeville star

Blazing City   **page 72**
A. 1. F   2. F   3. T   4. F   5. F
B. 1. C   2. I   3. I   4. C   5. C
C. 1. In Greek myth, only one phoenix lived at a time. After 500 years, the bird built a funeral pyre and burned itself to death. A new young bird then rose from the ashes.
   2. Nero was the corrupt emperor of Rome from A.D. 54 to A.D. 68. He burned his own city in order to build himself a new palace, then blamed the unpopular Christians, heightening their persecution from all sides.
   3. Answers will vary.

A Deadly Game   **page 73**
A. 1. e, 2. c, 3. a, 4. d, 5. b
B. Answers will vary.

Atomic Nightmare   **page 74**
A. Bikini Atoll; group of tiny islands in northwest Pacific, evacuated in 1945 for U.S. nuclear bomb tests. In 1968 the government okayed residents' return, but learned later the islands were still not safe. Three Mile Island: reactor in Harrisburg, Pennsylvania, where first nuclear accident occurred in 1979. Alerted public to need for extreme safety measures. Chernobyl: Soviet reactor where an explosion in 1986 released large amounts of radioactive material into atmosphere, causing deaths and serious illnesses. Positive uses of nuclear power: Communication—radio waves can transmit messages anywhere on earth. Fiber optics and satellites make use of nuclear technology. Industry—businesses use nuclear power to test materials and to produce heat that generates electricity. Scientific research uses nuclear technology to determine the dates of extremely old artifacts.

B., C., D. Answers will vary.

ANIMAL MAGNETISM
The Cat Conundrum   **page 76**
A. 1. g, 2. d, 3. f, 4. j, 5. c, 6. h, 7. i, 8. a, 9. e, 10. b
B. 1. conundrum   6. ruthless
   2. aura   7. vermin
   3. attribute   8. granary
   4. uncanny   9. feline
   5. aloof   10. wily
C. Graph should show these times: 3500 B.C., Use & Enjoy; 800 B.C., Worship; Middle Ages, Fear; 1600's, Use & Enjoy; today, Use & Enjoy.
D. 1. a quick nap
   2. a sophisticated person
   3. one who copies what others do
   4. a string game
   5. a narrow walkway
   6. a positive occurrence in a person's life
   7. a stealthy thief
   8. swamp plant with fuzzy brown stems
   9. a skittish person
   10. a downpour
   11. an ugly fight
   12. reveal a secret
E. 1. The cat in Egypt was a pampered pet. Over 300,000 cat mummies have been found. Bast, the Goddess of Love, had the head of a cat and the body of a woman. The modern Abyssinian cat is thought to have descended from those the ancient Egyptians kept.
   2. Other cat members are lion, tiger, panther, leopard. They are larger, stronger, and more ferocious in nature.
   3. Puss in Boots; Hey Diddle Diddle; St. Ives; Brementown Musicians

Ear to the Ground   **page 77**
A. 2
B. 1. bee   6. cat
   2. eagle   7. fish
   3. cow   8. pig
   4. dog   9. monkey
   5. horse   10. bear
C. 1. Icarus and his father, Daedalus, builder of the Cretan maze, designed wings made of wax and feathers. Icarus flew too near the sun, his wings melted, and he drowned in the sea.
   2. John James Audubon: 1785-1851, failed at many business efforts until he published his paintings of American birds, the first ever marketed.
   3. Roger Tory Peterson, 1908-1996, trained as an artist, developed a system of identifying birds by their distinguishing marks.

Sea Skimmers   **page 78**
A. 1. F, 2. F, 3. T, 4. F, 5. T, 6. T, 7. F, 8. F
B. Answers will vary.

The Garish Gar   **page 79**
A. 1. T, 2. F, 3. F, 4. F, 5. T, 6. F
B., C., D. Answers will vary.

Scorpion Secret page 80
A. 1. c 2. e 3. a 4. d 5. b
B. 1. c 2. e 3. a 4. d 5. b
C. Answers will vary.
D. Scorpio: Oct. 23-Nov. 21, secretive, intense, passionate

A Tail Tale page 82
A. 1. f, 2. e, 3. i, 4. h, 5. j, 6. b, 7. k, 8. a, 9. d, 10. g, 11. c
B. 1. I, 2. I, 3. C, 4. I, 5. C, 6. C, 7. I, 8. I, 9. C, 10. I, 11. C
C. Answers will vary.
D. 1. none 2. V 3. I 4. none 5. III 6. IV 7. II
E. 1. peacock
2. eagle
3. glass lizard, tree skink
4. dab lizard, sheep
5. woodpecker, monkey, chameleon
6. seahorse
7. Arctic fox
8. panther, frilled lizard
9. lion, Indian moon moth

Unlikely Mermaids page 84
A. 1. fourth 2. second 3. fifth 4. third 5. first
B. 1. Humans should avoid harmful contact with manatees.
2. Sirenians were not safe from humans even before motorized boating became popular.
3. Humans find the manatees' slow, gentle nature appealing.
4. Building in coastal areas should be carefully monitored to protect manatee waters.
C. Answers will vary.
D. 1. turkey 8. goose
2. swan 9. hare
3. beaver 10. bird
4. goat 11. kangaroo
5. fish 12. pigeon
6. pig 13. eel
7. hawk 14. oyster

Man's Best Friends page 86
A. 1. e, 2. c, 3. h, 4. f, 5. i, 6. a, 7. j, 8. d, 9. g, 10. b
B. 1, 2. Answers will vary.
3. Some elderly go back to childish behavior, wanting a doll, pouting, or crying easily.
4. Answers will vary.
5. A discriminating shopper checks quality and price to get good value.
6. Every wife would like a tame and useful husband!
7, 8. Answers will vary.
9. Farmers and greenskeepers have to break up clods, janitors have to clean them up when people track them inside.
10. Count to 10, punch a pillow, scream outside, play hard at a sport, sing.
C. 1. g, 2. g, 3. f, 4. e, 5. b, 6. d, 7. g, 8. e, 9. a, 10. d

Animal Metropolis page 87
A. 1. 400,000,000 prairie dogs; New York: 7,360,000; Chicago: 2,732,000; Los Angeles: 3,450,000.

2. protection, housing, convenient food, services, comfort
3. lack of food or room, presence of danger, inability to produce (find) adequate resources.
B. 1. pampas: Argentina, prairie: U.S., llanos: South America, veldt: Africa, steppe: Russia
2. Because there is no shelter in which to hide, some grassland animals are swift in order to outrun their enemies. Others tunnel underground for safety. Herd-living means safety in numbers.
C. Answers will vary.

Nature's Bristle Balls page 88
A. 1. F, 2. F, 3. T, 4. T, 5. F, 6. F, 7. F, 8. T, 9. T, 10. T
B., C. Answers will vary.

Here's to Ears! page 90
A. 1. acute 5. auditory
2. flaunt 6. instinctual
3. sedentary 7. Cartilage
4. impair 8. vulnerable
B. Diagram should show the auditory canal linking the outer auricle complete with lobe and muscle to the cochlea with mineral grains.
C. 1. T, 2. F, 3. T, 4. F, 5. T, 6. F
D., E. Answers will vary.

Whose Shoes? page 91
A. 4
B. 1. T, 2. F, 3. F, 4. T, 5. T, 6. F
C. 1. Hermaphroditus was the son of Hermes and Aphrodite whose body became joined into one body with a nymph.
2. The brig has two styles of sails united on one ship, square-rigged forward, schooner-rigged aft.
3. In the slipper, different organs function at different times. In the worm, both kinds of organs are active at once, but are located on different areas of the body.
4. Other shells include the bear claw, angel wing, moon shell, auger, lady's ear.
D. Answers will vary.

Unbelievable Bezoars page 92
A. 1. ball-shaped 2. pressed down 3. grass chewing
4. the process by which body fluids form a solid
5. returning to health 6. liquid medicine 7. poison
B. 1. F, 2. T, 3. F, 4. T, 5. T, 6. F
C., D. Answers will vary.

Friend in the Sea page 94
A. 4
B. Paragraph 1: Ever since the first boat ventured out to sea,
Paragraph 2: The dolphin has captured modern man's imagination as well,
C. Answers will vary.
D. 1. Dolphins have beaks, pointed teeth, and larger fins. Porpoises have no beaks, flat teeth, rounded heads, and smaller fins.
2. killer whales, pilot whales

3. Apollo took the form of a dolphin and led a lost ship safely to land. In gratitude, the sailors built a temple which they named in honor of the creature.
E. Answers will vary.
F. 1. c, 2. f, 3. e, 4. a, 5. d, 6. b, 7. g
G. 1. harbinger
   2. Aggressive
   3. humane
   4. lapped
   5. venture
   6. revere
   7. Aquatic

Itching to Know   page 96
A. 1. e, 2. d, 3. g, 4. b, 5. h, 6. j, 7. i, 8. a, 9. f, 10. c
B. Answers will vary.
C. The killing of
   1. self
   2. parents
   3. brother
   4. mother
   5. baby
   6. race of people
   7. a human
   8. sister
   9. father
   10. one's own child
D. The Buzz on Mosquito Bites
E. 1. T, 2. F, 3. F, 4. T, 5. T, 6. F, 7. T, 8. F, 9. F, 10. F

WHAT IN THE WORLD . . .?
Down and Dirty   page 98
A. 1. e, 2. i, 3. c, 4. g, 5. h, 6. a, 7. j, 8. f, 9. d, 10. b
B. 1. A, 2. S, 3. S, 4. A, 5. A, 6. S, 7. S, 8. A, 9. A
C. Diagram should show rock/particles mixing with decayed plant and animal material/soil/elements leaching from soil/water washing soil to ocean/pressure turning sediment into rock/rocks heaving above ground.
D. Answers will vary.
E. 1. They replaced deeply rooted prairie grass with less sturdy wheat fields and allowed their cattle to overgraze.
   2. They decay, mingling their nutrients with rock particles.
   3. Water first washes nutrients away, then washes soil into the ocean.
   4. Weathering over time turns volcanic rock into a rich soil suitable for growing pineapples.
   5. It is the black dirt of Russia, good for wheat.
F. 1. Common soil conservation practices: plowing in furrows to channel and hold water, planting trees as a windbreak, tilling cover crops under to feed the soil, rotating crops.
   2. The Netherlands uses a system of dikes and pumps (once powered by windmill) to recover land covered by the sea, forming a region known as the polders.
   3. The dust bowl, 1935-1938, damaged 100 million acres in Colorado, Kansas, New Mexico, Oklahoma, and Texas. Forty big storms hit in 1935 alone.

4. The sequoia, also know as the redwood, grows over 300 feet tall and 10 feet in diameter. Now only 70 groves of these thousand-year-old trees grow along the Pacific coastal fog belt.

Quite a Charge!   page 100
A. 1. e, 2. d, 3. f, 4. b, 5. a, 6. c, 7. g
B. 1. no, they are both browned on the outside.
   2. The Country Mouse and the City Mouse
   3. Answers will vary.
   4. to comfort those who lose
   5. Answers will vary.
C. 1. III, 2. none, 3. I, 4. IV, 5. none, 6. II
D. Answers will vary.
E. 1. 100
   2. 1,000
   3. 30
   4. 30,000,000
   5. 10,000
   6. 60,000
   7. 10
   8. 7
   9. 8,000,000

Surrealist Scene   page 101
A. 3
B. Answers will vary.
C. 1. d, 2. h, 3. f, 4. c, 5. a, 6. j, 7. g, 8. i, 9. b, 10. e

A Losing Battle   page 102
A. 1. d, 2. c, 3. e, 4. a, 5. b
B. Answers will vary.
C. 2
D. Western Sahara, Egypt, Morocco, Algeria, Tunisia, Libya, Sudan, Chad, Niger, Mali, Mauritania
E., F. Answers will vary.

Floating Flowers   page 104
A. 1. tourists traveling to visit bed of lilies near Chicago
   2. a waterlily
   3. an Egyptian tomb painter
   4. jacana
   5. Monet
   6. a waterlily stalk
B. Answers will vary.
C. 1. Claude Monet: 1840-1926, painted his first spontaneous impressions of landscapes.
   2. The jacana is a small, tropical, wading bird that runs over lily leaves, eating bugs.
   3. The lotus was held sacred and immortal in Egypt because of its association with the life-giving Nile. Lilies would bloom seemingly overnight from a bed that had been dry just days before.
D. Answers will vary.
E. 1. F, 2. T, 3. F, 4. F, 5. F, 6. F, 7. T, 8. T, 9. F, 10. T

Desert Tall Tale   page 105
A. 1. C, 2. C, 3. I, 4. C, 5. I
B. 1. world's record for height
   2. yes
   3. no
   4. swells with absorbed rain

C. 1. Because the saguaro's branches are covered with tough ridges, water does not evaporate quickly.
    2. The saguaro grows so slowly, thieves could easily wipe out the entire species before new ones could grow.
D., E. Answers will vary.

Northern Lights   page 106
A. No matter how science and legend differ,
B. 1. C, 2. C, 3. I, 4. C, 5. I
C. Diagram should show wind pushing particles from sun to earth, over North Pole, particles hit atmosphere and release energy.
D. 1. Mars, god of war
    2. Somnus, god of sleep
    3. Ceres, goddess of grain
    4. Vulcan, god of fire
    5. Hypnog, god of sleep
    6. Helios, sun god

The Other Rain Forest   page 108
A. 1. g, 2. c, 3. f, 4. e, 5. h, 6. a, 7. d, 8. i, 9. j, 10. b
B. 1. crevice
    2. lush
    3. vascular
    4. deciduous
    5. emerge
    6. migratory
    7. nestle
    8. canopy
    9. invertebrate
    10. lichens
C. 1. Trop   7. Trop
    2. B   8. Temp
    3. Temp   9. B
    4. Temp   10. Temp
    5. Trop   11. Trop
    6. B   12. Temp

Curious Carnivore   page 110
A. 1. c, 2. b, 3. d, 4. f, 5. a, 6. e
B. Answers will vary.
C. 1. carnivore: wolf, otter, jackal, hyena, lion; herbivore: cow, earthworm, deer, horse; omnivore: bear, brown rat, opossum
    2. Both have leaves that close. Mimosa closes its leaves as a response to touch. Venus flytrap closes its leaves to trap meat to feed itself.
D. 1. F, 2. T, 3. F, 4. T, 5. F
E. Chart should show plant kingdom characterized by photosynthesis and no capacity for rapid movement; animal kingdom characterized by rapid response to stimulus, with Venus flytrap in between.
F. a. 5, b. 1, c. 4, d. 2, e. 3
G. Answers will vary.

The Tide That Towers   page 111
A. 1. 3
    2. 5
    3. 2
    4. 1
    5. 4
B. 1. bear: an animal, to carry; rest: the remainder, to relax; bark: the covering of a tree, the sound a dog makes; blow: to push air through the lips, a hit; purse: a wallet, to pucker the lips; till: a box for money, to plow; wind: breeze, to wrap up
    2. berth, groan, allowed, peal, coarse, bury, minor, cellar, flour, chews, serial, colonel, site, cite, bear, fare
C. Orellana's journey spanned the entire breadth of South America. He faced sickness and starvation, an attack from a tribe of female warriors, and became governor of the territory.

Sand Trap   page 112
A. 1. T, 2. F, 3. F, 4. F, 5. F
B. These words originally meant:
    1. happy, then weak or sickly
    2. peasant
    3. bold, brave
    4. crafty
    5. servant
    6. chancy
C. 1. Roanoke was established in 1587 by Sir Walter Raleigh and 117 settlers. A ship went to England for supplies and, returning, found all traces of the colony gone.
    2. The Wright brothers tested the first successful airplane at windy Kitty Hawk on Dec. 17, 1903.
    3. Blackbeard terrorized the North Carolina and Virginia coasts during 1717 and 1718. He came ashore on the Outer Banks frequently and it is rumored that he buried treasure here.

Recess for Rocks   page 114
A. 4
B. Answers will vary.
C. 1. 4
    2. 2
    3. 5
    4. 3
    5. 1
D., E. Answers will vary.
F. 1. F, 2. T, 3. T, 4. F, 5. F